THE IDEA OF POVERTY

Paul Spicker

First published in Great Britain in 2007 by

The Policy Press
University of Bristol
Fourth Floor
Beacon House
Queen's Road
Bristol BS8 1QU
UK

Tel +44 (0)117 331 4054
Fax +44 (0)117 331 4093
e-mail tpp-info@bristol.ac.uk
www.policypress.org.uk

© Paul Spicker 2007

British Library Cataloguing in Publication Data
A catalogue record for this book is available from the British Library.

Library of Congress Cataloging-in-Publication Data
A catalog record for this book has been requested.

ISBN 978 1 86134 888 3 paperback
ISBN 978 1 86134 889 0 hardcover

Cover design by Qube Design Associates, Bristol.
Printed and bound in Great Britain by MPG Books, Bodmin.

Contents

Preface   iv
Acknowledgements   vii
About the author   viii

Part One: Understanding poverty   1
one   Defining poverty   3
two   Poverty in different societies   11
three   Understanding the figures   19

Part Two: Poverty as material need   27
four   Concepts of need   29
five   Area deprivation   37

Part Three: Poverty as economic position   43
six   Economic resources   45
seven   Class   53

Part Four: Poverty and social relationships   63
eight   Social exclusion   65
nine   Dependency   73
ten   Poverty and politics   83

Part Five: Poverty as a moral concept   91
eleven   The moral dimensions of poverty   93
twelve   The moral condemnation of the poor   101

Part Six: Explanations for poverty   109
thirteen Why people are poor   111
fourteen Why poor countries stay poor   121

Part Seven: Responses to poverty   133
fifteen Responding to poverty   135
sixteen Policies for poverty   143

Notes   153
Index   173

Preface

This book examines views about what poverty is and what should be done about it. Poverty refers to a complex set of ideas, which mean different things to different people – for example, material deprivation, lack of money, dependency on benefits, social exclusion or inequality. The nature and meaning of poverty is disputed. Some people argue that poverty has a different character in the industrialised countries of the West from the deprived areas of the developing world. Some would go further, to argue that the nature of poverty differs, not just between rich and poor countries, but between and within countries – a position which makes comparisons and generalisations profoundly difficult. The structure of the book, and a large part of its agenda, is based on an exploration of the meaning and implications of different understandings of poverty.

The book is not only an examination of meaning, however. The way we understand poverty affects the kinds of problems we recognise, and it is hard to separate interpretations of poverty from views about what ought to be done. In theory, the issues ought to be separable. In practice, discussions of poverty are often muddled, emotional and strongly disputed.

I can show this most effectively with an example. The ideas considered in this book cover both rich and poor countries, but it is in the developed world that the concept of poverty is most disputed. Imagine Anne, a single parent with two children, living in Britain. She separated from her partner three years ago, and has had no contact with him since. She lives mainly on social assistance benefits, though her income is dependent on a range of other social provisions such as tax credits, Child Benefit and Housing Benefit. Anne lives in public housing, in a tenement block built in the 1950s. The apartment is spartan; it has three bedrooms, kitchen and bathroom, and although the property is in good repair it tends to be damp in winter because she cannot afford the heating. She shops for food once a week at the local supermarket. She cannot afford to go out for meals or drinks, and she does not go out very much. She generally stays at home and watches television. Anne tries to manage, but the amount of money available on benefit is very small, and she often finds herself with no money at the end of a fortnight.

Is Anne poor? People who are faced with that question tend to answer it in one of four ways. The first answer is to say that yes, she is poor. That answer would be given by many social researchers in this field. Anne is on a low income; she is on benefits; she is socially isolated; her housing is basic; her choices and opportunities are limited. She does not have enough to participate in the society around her.

The second answer is to say that no, she is not poor. Anne is typical of many people living in Britain. Britain is, by most standards, a wealthy country. Anne has a secure tenancy. The house may be damp, but it is wind- and weather-tight, and that is not true of housing for poor people in many countries. The standard of housing is high by comparison with most countries of the world. Every house has an internal water supply, including a supply of drinking water, and an inside toilet. External facilities like roads, sanitation, foul water removal and storm drainage are the norm rather than the exception. Every house provided by social housing has an electricity supply, hot water, central heating and separate kitchen and bathroom facilities; the main problems lie in paying for fuel rather than having access to it at all. If Anne lives in social housing, and shops once a week, it is safe to assume that she has somewhere to store food. She has a television, which some people think is a luxury. Her children will be able to go to school; if they are sick, there will be medical care available. For people who doubt whether Anne is poor, poverty consists of many worse forms of deprivation. There are people in developing countries who have no food, no water and no sanitation. By comparison, Anne is positively well off. John Moore, a former Conservative minister of social security, once launched a ringing attack on the 'poverty lobby' in the UK for claiming that this kind of situation represents poverty. 'These people', Moore said, 'would find poverty in Paradise'.

The third answer is to say that 'there is not enough information here'. What resources does Anne have? How does she live? What are her relationships with other people? How long has she been in this position? What are her prospects? If poverty is only about a person's income, or based in material needs such as access to water supplies, we do not need to know all this. If we need to know this kind of thing before we can decide whether someone is poor, it is because poverty is defined in terms of something other than need or resources – issues like opportunities, prospects, or relationships. If these questions are appropriate – as many people think they are – the definition of poverty goes rather beyond needs, income or a person's standard of living.

The fourth response is a different kind of answer. Many people will have looked at the details and asked, not whether Anne is poor, but what our response to her circumstances should be. People who support the poor might ask: should Anne not have a better safety net? Why are the benefits not more adequate? How can we justify a system where people don't have money for food? People who disapprove might ask: where is the children's father? What is he doing? Is it Anne's fault? Should she be getting benefits? Shouldn't she be managing better? These arguments, on both sides, do not really address the question of whether Anne is poor – they seem to go off at a tangent – but they are heard so frequently in discussions of poverty that they cannot be ignored. They overlap with the decision about whether or not Anne should be described as poor. When people talk about 'poverty', they are often not trying to make a simple, descriptive statement about a social issue. Hidden in the idea of 'poverty' is the idea that *something must be done*. When people really want to say that 'something must be done', they find ways of saying it. They say that people are poor, they are deprived, they are being denied their rights, and so on. Conversely, when people don't want to accept that something should be done, they try to find ways of saying that it shouldn't be. This can be done by saying that people are not poor, or that if they are poor it's their own fault and none of our business.

Issues which seem, at first sight, to be about definition often go beyond that. *The idea of poverty* examines, not just how poverty is defined, but the normative dimensions of the idea – the moral status of the poor, the causes of poverty and responses to poverty. The agenda for this book, then, is a mixture of descriptive and normative understandings of poverty. The book aims to discuss:

- how the idea of poverty can be understood;
- the kinds of conditions associated with poverty, and how poverty affects the lives of poor people;
- the reasons why people are poor; and
- how we should respond.

The idea of poverty should help readers to make sense of a wide range of conflicting and contradictory source material. But it is also written from a committed perspective. It argues for inclusive understandings of poverty, and it challenges some of the myths and common stereotypes about poverty and the poor.

Paul Spicker
Centre for Public Policy and Management
The Robert Gordon University

Acknowledgements

I have drawn some of the arguments in this book from previously published papers. I should like to thank the publishers for permission to reuse parts of my own written material.

- The argument and Figure 1.1 in Chapter One is based on P Spicker, 1999, 'Definitions of poverty: eleven clusters of meaning', in D Gordon and P Spicker (eds) *The international glossary on poverty*, London: Zed Books.
- Chapter Three takes sections on 'Measuring poverty' and 'Presenting indicators' from P Spicker, 2004, 'Developing indicators: issues in the use of quantitative data about poverty', *Policy & Politics*, 32(4), pp 431-40.
- Chapter Five is drawn from P Spicker, 2001, 'Poor areas and the "ecological fallacy"', *Radical Statistics*, 76, pp 38-79, available at: www.radstats.org.uk/journal.htm
- Chapter Eight includes material from P Spicker, 1997, 'Exclusion', *Journal of Common Market Studies*, 35(1), pp 133-43.
- Short sections in Chapters Nine and Thirteen are drawn from P Spicker, 2002, *Poverty and the welfare state*, London: Catalyst.

However, because the book is aimed at a general readership, none of these sections is reproduced in its original form.

About the author

Paul Spicker holds the Grampian Chair of Public Policy at the Robert Gordon University, Aberdeen, and is Director of the Centre for Public Policy and Management. His research includes studies of poverty, need, disadvantage and service delivery; he has worked as a consultant for a range of agencies in social welfare provision. His books include:

Stigma and social welfare (Croom Helm, 1984)
Principles of social welfare (Routledge, 1988)
Social housing and the social services (Longman, 1989)
Poverty and social security: concepts and principles (Routledge, 1993)
Social policy: themes and approaches (Prentice Hall, 1995)
Planning for the needs of people with dementia (with D S Gordon, Avebury, 1997)
Social protection: a bilingual glossary (co-edited with J-P Révauger, Mission-Recherche, 1998)
Social policy in a changing society (with Maurice Mullard, Routledge, 1998)
The international glossary on poverty (co-editor with David Gordon, Zed Books, 1999)
The welfare state: a general theory (Sage Publications, 2000).
Policy analysis for practice: applying social policy (The Policy Press, 2006)
Liberty, equality and fraternity (The Policy Press, 2006)

Part One
Understanding poverty

ONE

Defining poverty

This book explores the different meanings of poverty and the views that people hold about it. Although the book is written as an introduction to ideas about poverty, it is unlikely that anyone who reads it will have no prior thoughts about what 'poverty' might mean. If the way the book deals with the subject does not fit with the way that readers understand the issues, it will probably seem to miss the point. From the perspective of someone who thinks that poverty is about malnutrition and destitution in developing countries, a study of how people live in the *banlieues* of Paris or a housing scheme in Glasgow is likely to seem marginally relevant at best. If poverty is about how people live, the vast literature on measuring low income may seem irrelevent. If poverty is all about low income, a discussion of social problems might look like a distraction – poverty might lead to problems, but that is not the main issue. And where people think that poverty is about social problems, focusing on malnutrition and destitution offers a very narrow perspective on a much wider set of questions. The various understandings of poverty are often inconsistent, and there is no easy way to reconcile them all.

The best way to understand what a term means is not usually to start with a definition, because people mean different things by the same words. Long ago, philosophers used to define things in terms of 'essence' and 'attributes'. If we wanted to define a term, it would have an 'essence', something at the core, and we could detect it by looking at the way it appeared, and working out what the thing really was. If this was right, it would be possible to look at the problems of poverty – issues like malnutrition, bad housing, or low income – and work out what poverty was from that. But this approach does not work even for simple ideas, and it certainly does not work for the idea of poverty. Poverty doesn't have an 'essence'. It means many things. By some accounts it means something different everywhere, in every society. The nature of poverty is contested. There isn't a simple, single consistent way of explaining what poverty is.

Words that are widely used acquire a range of inter-related meanings. This approach to deciphering meaning was pioneered by the philosopher, Ludwig Wittgenstein. The example that Wittgenstein uses is the word 'game', which means many things – for example, a childish pastime, a contest, a sport, or the product of hunting. Each of the meanings of the word is linked by a 'family resemblance' to others, but the link between the first and the last meaning in the chain is fairly remote.[3] The same principle applies to many words, and the idea of 'poverty' is complex in the same way. There is not one meaning of 'poverty', but many. There are clusters of meaning, rather than firm and clear understandings, and the link between the clusters is sometimes difficult to see.

There are scores of different definitions of poverty, but within the many definitions there are eleven main clusters of meaning. This book looks at the main clusters in some detail, but for the purposes of an initial discussion it will be helpful to identify the classes of definition here.

Poverty refers, in the first instance, to **material need**. This includes three main types of definition:

- Poverty as *specific need*, where people lack certain things that are essential to them. It is possible to find references, and indeed political campaigns, about 'food poverty', 'fuel poverty' or 'housing poverty'. When people lack the things they need, they are said to be deprived.
- Poverty as a *pattern of deprivation*. Poverty, to some, is not about what people lack; it is a general condition where people are in need in various ways over an extended period of time, past, present and future. People are not poor, by this account, because they are living in bad housing; they are poor if they have been there for some time and can't get out of it.
- Poverty as a *low standard of living*. People who have low income or consumption over a period of time have to make do with less than others.

The second main group of definitions sees poverty as a description of people's **economic circumstances**. There are again three main categories:

- Poverty as a *lack of resources*. People are said to be poor if they do not have the resources to obtain the things they want. (The lack of resources is the definition of poverty; need is the result.)
- Poverty as *economic distance*. If people have less resources than other people, they cannot afford the things that other people can afford. Where there is a competition for scarce resources, such as land or housing, they cannot afford them, even if their income is higher than other people's elsewhere. Economic distance means that people cannot afford to live where they are.
- Poverty as *economic class*. A 'class' in economic terms is determined by people's relationship to the system of production. The economic position of (for example) marginal workers, older people and disabled people means that they are not able to command resources in many societies, and that they are likely to be poor.

Third, there are **social relationships**. Here, there are four categories:

- *Social class*. People's social position depends on a combination of economic position, educational attainment and social status. Poverty, for many, refers to the position of the lowest class, people who lack status, power and opportunities available to others.
- *Dependency*. For some, poverty is defined as dependency on social assistance or 'welfare' – the link between benefits and poverty is taken for granted, and no distinction is made in the press between receiving benefits and being poor.

- *Social exclusion.* This is a confusing term, widely used in the European Union. It refers to people who are excluded from society – people who are left out, shut out or pushed out. It classifies together, then, people who are unable to participate in society because of poverty, vulnerable people who are not protected adequately (like asylum seekers and disabled people), and people who are socially rejected (like AIDS sufferers and drug users).
- *Lack of entitlement.* Amartya Sen, who has won the Nobel Prize for Economics, argues that poverty is best understood, not as lack of goods, but as lack of entitlement.[4] If Sen is right, poverty is not about resources as such: it is about legal, social and political arrangements. This view has been profoundly influential in the United Nations, where one of the core views is that poverty is linked to 'lack of basic security', understood in terms of people's rights.

This list has outlined ten main categories. The eleventh, which was touched on in the Preface, is a different way of understanding poverty. Beyond any of these categories, poverty is also a moral concept. When we say that people are 'poor', we are not just saying that they are in need, suffering hardship or disadvantaged: we are saying that it is serious, and that something should be done.

These are clusters of meaning, rather than definitions in themselves. Each of them refers to several different ways of looking at the issues of poverty, and there are competing definitions in each of them. Some well-known definitions, like Townsend's idea of 'relative deprivation'[5], or Paugam's 'social disqualification'[6], cut across many of the categories at the same time. The clusters are not very sharply defined; each of them overlaps with some of the others. Figure 1.1 shows this material in the form of a diagram. Each definition is similar to the meanings next to it, and there are some links across the circle – for example, lack of resources is closely linked to lack of entitlement. However, as we move around the circle, the definitions grow further apart. Lack of entitlement is very different from economic distance; dependency is not the same as a low standard of living; patterns of deprivation cannot simply be identified with economic class. The normative concept – the view of poverty as unacceptable hardship – lies at the centre, because all the other concepts are linked directly to that kind of normative evaluation.

Most of this book is taken up with discussion and explanations of these concepts. Part Two looks at material conditions; Part Three at economic circumstances; Part Four at social relationships; and Part Five, at the moral elements in the idea of poverty.

Scientific and participatory definitions of poverty

Currently, there are two dominant schools of thought as to how poverty can best be understood. The first is represented by the work of economists and

Figure 1.1: Family resemblances between different concepts of poverty

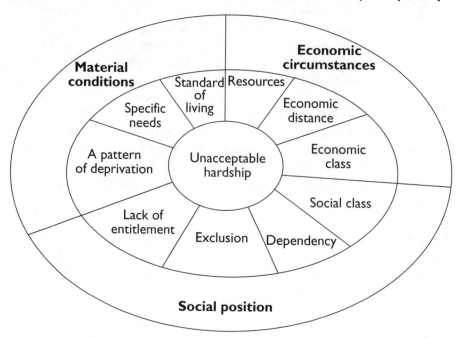

Source: P Spicker, 1999, 'Definitions of poverty: eleven clusters of meaning', in D Gordon and P Spicker (eds) *The international glossary on poverty*, London: Zed Books. Reproduced with permission.

social scientists across the world. A declaration signed by Peter Townsend and many of the leading researchers in the field put the following argument to international organisations:

> EUROPEAN SOCIAL SCIENTISTS are critical of the unwillingness at international level to introduce a cross-country and therefore more scientific operational definition of poverty. In recent years, a variety of different definitions have been reviewed and evaluated. They apply only to countries or groups of countries. Many are conceptually unclear: some confuse cause and effect. ... Poverty is primarily an income- or resource-driven concept. It is more than having a relatively low income. ... If criteria independent of income can be further developed and agreed, measures of the severity and extent of the phenomenon of poverty can be properly grounded. That will lead to better investigation of cause and more reliable choice of priorities in policy. SCIENTIFIC PROGRESS can be made if material deprivation is also distinguished from both social deprivation and social exclusion. ... All countries should introduce international measures of these basic concepts and take immediate steps to improve

the accepted meanings, measurement and explanation of poverty, paving the way for more effective policies.[7]

There are some questionable assertions here – for example, it is debatable whether poverty is 'primarily' about income and resources – but they are not what the declaration is mainly about. The central point is that poverty is capable of being understood and analysed scientifically. If it can be taken as having a clear meaning, it can be measured, its relationship with other issues can be pinned down, and it can be responded to accordingly. Social science mainly works by tracking relationships between different issues. If, for example, we identify poor health or low educational attainment as problems associated with low income, we can work out what are the circumstances in which those relationships hold, which measures improve the situation, and which do not. That is how a clearer understanding can lead to more effective policy.

Poverty is one of the most researched and analysed subjects in social science. Some of the research tries to identify poverty, some to measure it, and some to explain it. Although the argument for scientific analysis is strong, there are problems with it. The trouble is not that poverty cannot be analysed; it is that 'poverty' means many different things. In practical terms, this means that when researchers try to analyse poverty, they are only able to identify a part of it at a time. So, we can find cases where important issues like housing conditions or social exclusion are put to one side because it is difficult to fit them into the analysis. In some cases, the methods used to identify poverty drive the debate to such an extent that they change the way the subject is understood. Research on poverty has been dominated by issues like household budgets, income or benefit receipt, because they are easier to measure than problems in personal development or social relationships, and they may seem less easy to dispute.

The main competing school of thought has grown out of work in developing countries, and it sees poverty as many-sided. Like the Hydra in the Greek myth, poverty has many heads, and if you cut off one of them it grows again. The previous section described three main categories of definition: material needs, economic circumstances and social relationships. Poverty refers to needs, to the things that people do not have – food, shelter, and security. It refers to the economic power they have, including income, resources and their role in the economy. And it refers to social issues, including social rights, exclusion and participation in society. All of these issues can be analysed, but they are all problematic. Dealing with part of them does not mean that they are dealt with completely. Dealing with one or more does not mean that all of them are being dealt with.

The multidimensional view has profound implications for policy. Seeing poverty as many issues, rather than one, lends itself to a different kind of approach. The way to deal with a complex, intractable set of problems is to break them down into smaller, more manageable problems. If the smaller problems are still too difficult, they have to be broken down in turn. Eventually we will end up with many problems, but problems we stand some chance of dealing with.

The trouble with this approach is that, at times, it seems that there are just too many problems to deal with. It has the potential to become a counsel of despair: the problem of poverty is too big, too complicated and too awkward to deal with. How can we sensibly decide which issues to deal with, when there are so many, and they are so serious? The view that is increasingly being taken in studies in developing countries is that if 'we' means the decision makers, politicians and economists engaged with these problems, 'we' can't. Faced with a large set of awkward, conflicting issues, the best approach is not to decide; it is to ask people who are poor what matters to them, and to take those issues as the priorities.

This is the philosophy behind *Voices of the poor*, a set of studies undertaken by the World Bank.[8] *Voices of the poor* is one of the best studies ever written on the subject of poverty. It is based on large numbers of interviews with groups of people; more than 20,000 subjects participated in 23 countries during the course of 1999. It reports the feelings and concerns of poor people in their own words. Statements from people in different cultures are classified and brought together, and a range of recurring themes are identified. The first volume, *Can anyone hear us?*, has a rich vein of material, the authentic voice of poor people and a developed structure to make the material accessible. It is not easy to read, however: the comments of poor people are strongly rooted in their different cultures, and the idea, for example, that 'the pig is the woman's cow', may be just too gnomic to hit home. The second volume, *Crying out for change*, chooses themes based on the common concerns of poor people. The kinds of theme it identifies – precarious livelihoods, lack of security and limited participation in society – are immediately recognisable across a range of experience.

The view of poverty which emerges from the study is multifaceted (see Box 1). It is in the nature of participatory research that definitions flow from the way in which people use concepts themselves, not from the imposition of definitions from above. Irresistibly, with such a large number of participants, this leads to many different understandings of the idea of poverty. It may be that the issues which poor people point to are not the issues that other people think of as part of 'poverty'. The issues still matter to the people they affect. This is not just about definitions; it is also about empowering the poor. Commitment to a multidimensional view of poverty is, then, a moral position.

A participatory approach does not exclude scientific approaches, but it does limit their scope. There is no real hope of finding an 'answer' to poverty, anywhere or ever. There is not one issue to find an answer to. The best we can hope for is to deal with a few of the problems at a time. The participatory approach sets the framework, and makes it possible to understand the scope of the problems and the importance of the issues. The scientific approach then makes it possible to focus on a particular problem, and to see what works and what does not.

Box 1: *Voices of the poor*

Poverty as material need

'Don't ask me what poverty is because you have met it outside my house. Look at the house and count the number of holes. Look at my utensils and the clothes that I am wearing. Look at everything and write what you see. What you see is poverty.' (Kenya)

'They [the children] sometimes just get sick for no reason. Sometimes it's because of lack of food. We are poor. We have no money to buy or to feed ourselves.' (Ecuador)

Poverty as economic position

'It's the cost of living, low salaries, and lack of jobs.' (Brazil)

'A poor person is a person who does not own anything that provides him with a permanent source of living. If a person has a permanent source of income, he will not ask for other people's assistance.' (Egypt)

'You have to have a job. Where are the job opportunities?' (Scotland)

Poverty as social relationships

'Poverty is humiliation, the sense of being dependent on them, and of being forced to accept rudeness, insults, and indifference when we seek help.' (Latvia)

'Poverty is lack of freedom, enslaved by crushing daily burden, by depression and fear of what the future will bring.' (Georgia)

Sources: D Narayan, 1999, *Voices of the poor: Can anyone hear us?*, Oxford: Oxford University Press/World Bank; D Narayan, R Chambers, M Shah and P Petesch, 2000, *Voices of the Poor: Crying out for change*, Oxford: Oxford University Press/World Bank; Dundee Anti-Poverty Forum, 2003, *No room for dreams*, Dundee: Dundee Anti-Poverty Forum.

Debates about poverty are usually selective, and they are likely to leave out issues which matter to people. I have acted as mentor in a couple of participatory local projects where volunteer workers, including people who themselves were in poverty, aimed to get a sense of other poor people's concerns.[9] Some of those concerns were wholly predictable – issues like low income and lack of opportunity in the job market. Some were unsurprising, given a small degree of local knowledge: people were concerned about transport and child care. But some of the issues raised were unexpected in the context of a discussion of poverty, like concerns about pets and deafness. It is too easy to say that 'this is not really about poverty'. Ignoring issues that don't fit our preconceptions diminishes the seriousness of the issues for the people who experience them. In the course of this book, I cannot hope to review every topic that people think might be an issue of poverty, but I can make an argument for a generally inclusive approach. Although much of the material is appropriate for people who want to learn more about the subject, I should attach a warning: I argue for particular positions, and the book is committed, rather than even-handed. Part of my aim here is to make converts. I do not expect anyone to agree with everything in the book, but even if you agree with only a small part of it, that small part will be leading you in the direction of a multidimensional view of poverty.

TWO

Poverty in different societies

I expect that many of the readers of this book will be people in developed countries – which is why, in the Preface, I used an example drawn from experience in Britain. This book, though, is about the idea of poverty, not poverty in any one country. The experience of poverty in the developed world can be very different to the developing countries where most of the world's poor live. Disputes about the meaning of poverty often boil down to a simple argument: that 'poverty' does not seem to mean the same thing in industrialised countries as it does in developing ones. At a superficial level, this is obviously true. Poverty has many different forms, and it does not mean the same thing for people in a single country. It must be true, then, that it is not going to imply the same experience in different countries. If the statement means anything, it has to be saying something rather more weighty than this. People who hold that poverty is different in rich and poor countries are saying that different standards are being applied – that what passes for poverty in a rich country would not pass for poverty in a poor one.

There are two contexts in which this argument is commonly made. The first is among people in the richer countries who do not think that the problems of richer countries should be described in terms of 'poverty'. The second is found in international organisations, who aim to target their work on the people in greater need, and do not think that the same claims can be made by people in richer countries. The United Nations Development Programme (UNDP) produces a Human Poverty Index (HPI) every year, comparing aspects of the quality of life in different countries.[10] It uses two standards – HPI-1 for developing countries, and HPI-2 for developed ones. HPI-1 treats life expectancy as low when it falls below 40. HPI-2 treats life expectancy as low when it falls below 60. The two indices mean that poor countries are only to be compared to other poor countries, and richer countries to other rich countries. This is – literally – a double standard. It is not based on differences in needs; it is based in the idea that poor countries cannot sensibly be compared to rich ones. Although it may reflect genuine differences between countries, at least some part of it seems to be based on assumptions about the way poverty needs to be presented.

The idea that poverty means the same thing in different countries is sometimes referred to as an 'absolute' concept of poverty, while the idea that it means different things is called 'relative' poverty. The debate between them generates rather more heat than light. For writers on development, such as Michael Lipton[11], 'absolute poverty' can be a way of drawing attention to the fundamental deprivations of people in the developing world, a set of problems we should be concerned about as a matter of common humanity. For other writers, notably Peter Townsend, 'absolute' poverty is associated with a minimalist, reductionist view of poverty. It is reductionist because it seems to him to ignore the issues of lifestyle, social relationships and the ability to participate in society; it is minimalist because it has been used to justify minimal social benefits and a narrow focus on issues like nutrition.[12] The distinction between 'absolute' and 'relative' concepts is not straightforward, however, and over time some of the most influential writers in the field have come to think that it is not as crucial to the debate as they used to believe.

Absolute poverty; basic needs

'Absolute poverty' has been explained as:

> a level of minimum need, below which people are regarded as poor, for the purpose of social and government concern, and which does not change over time.[13]

By this definition, poverty is absolute when it is fixed, constant and the same for everyone.

The core of the 'absolute' concept is the view that there is a minimum standard that everyone ought to have. This minimum standard is referred to, in documents from the UN and other international organisations, as 'basic needs'. The Copenhagen Declaration states:

> absolute poverty is a condition characterised by severe deprivation of basic human needs, including food, safe drinking water, sanitation facilities, health, shelter, education and information.[14]

On the face of the matter, this looks like a universal minimum. Scratching the surface, the position is not so clear. Everyone needs 'food', but the test of what can be considered to be food changes from one society to another. Diets change in different societies. In Britain, we do not eat horse-meat or snails; in France, people do. Many people, across the world, are unable to digest cow's milk: when, in the period after the Second World War, the US arranged for dried milk to be provided to help people in poor countries, it made them sick. The nature of 'education' and 'information' are clearly social, and if there are universal standards, it is not very clear what they should be. 'Shelter' seems straightforward, but what passes for shelter is different in different societies.

In each society, there are *norms* – not 'averages', but expectations and rules about how people ought to live. Take, for example, the issue of homelessness (see Box 2). Homelessness means, on the face of the matter, that people have nowhere to live. The position is not always straightforward, because many people

Box 2: Housing and homelessness

Homelessness is a residual problem – what happens to those who are left when there is not enough land or housing, or when some people are denied or excluded. It is not a single issue, and the experience is different in different contexts. In some countries, there is a core problem of rights to land: people who have no rights or access to land cannot build temporary shelters for themselves. This is true in some rich countries (like Britain and the US) as well as in some less developed ones (like India). In other countries, squatting on unclaimed land is a normal form of tenure – and squatter settlements can be seen not just in the poorest countries, but in some fairly developed ones, like the countries of southern Europe.

In other countries, the problem is based in lack of rights to housing rather than just land. Table 2.1 shows the pattern of housing tenure in cities in developing countries.[15] About a third of developing countries do not give people rights against eviction. Women lack rights to ownership, particularly in Africa and the Arab states, and there can be problems in obtaining mortgages where property is held in common, such as property in tribal lands.[16]

Table 2.1: Urban housing tenure in developing countries (%)

	Owned	Mort-gaged	Private rent	Social housing	Sub-tenant	Other	Squatter	Homeless
Africa	40.8	3.4	31.3	5.2	4.5	9.3	1.0	4.5
Asia-Pacific	61.4	3.6	23.4	0.9	0.3	2.1	1.5	6.8
Latin America	60.6	5.5	19.2	3.1	0.9	6.6	2.9	1.2
Former Eastern bloc	60.7	2.6	4.4	25.0	0.3	2.9	1.2	2.9
All developing countries	57.1	4.0	17.2	10.3	1.4	5.1	1.6	4.3

The key issues are, then, issues about:
- access and rights to land
- access and rights to accommodation; and
- access and rights to tenure.

These present very different problems. What they have in common is a focus on entitlement, which will be examined in Chapter Ten.

who have nowhere to live move from pillar to post – they spend time with friends, relatives, spend some time in hostels, some time out on the street, and so forth – but for the purposes of this argument, we can confine the discussion to people who have no shelter at all, and have to live on the street. This is not a problem which occurs across the world, because 'having to live on the street' takes on a different meaning in different locations. In some areas of the world, particularly in Africa and Latin America, squatting is a normal pattern of living. People who have nowhere to live build shelters for themselves, tacked together from such materials as are available. Street homelessness is a special case: it happens, not just when people are not able to gain access to normal housing, but when they are not able to squat. This is usually because the land is already claimed by someone else, as it is in much of the developed world, or in places like India where there is a structured system of landholding. There are other examples of street homelessness, like the street children of several Latin American cities, but they are further examples of cases where people are not able to squat. If we look at the problem of homelessness in developed countries, like the US, it needs to be understood in a particular social context. There are rules which govern where people can live, where they can stay, and what kind of shelters people are allowed to construct. The norms are different in different countries; but the circumstances which result are similar. We can say, quite sensibly, that people are 'homeless' in America just as they are 'homeless' in India.

Amartya Sen argues that we need to distinguish people's needs from the options that people have to meet those needs. If someone needs to eat, that need can be met in several ways. There are various *commodities*, or things, which have the *characteristic* that they can be used as food. Commodities and characteristics, Sen suggests, are socially defined; the basic need, or *capability* of the person to do things, may not be.[17] The problem with that formulation is that the things people need are also often social in nature. 'The capability of moving in a certain way', which is how Sen describes transport, means different things in different places. People 'need' transport only in a society where the ability to travel for a distance is required. Absolute poverty has to be understood, then, in a specific social context. It is not 'fixed', and it cannot be 'constant'. It can, however, be common to everyone, or 'universal'. The UNDP's decision to use different standards for death rates runs against that, but life expectancy is surely one of the areas where we can reasonably apply the same standards to poor countries as to rich ones. There are some problems which can be seen from the point of view of common humanity.

Relative poverty

The idea of 'relative poverty' means that poverty has to be understood in the context of the society where it happens. This means several things at once. In the first place, relative poverty has been used to mean simply that poverty is socially defined. That is beyond question, because the norms which lead to people being poor are social: what counts as food, clothing or shelter depends on the society you live in. This is part of any understanding of poverty, but the other implications of the idea of relative poverty go further.

The second meaning of 'relative poverty' is that poverty reflects social inequality. This has been referred to before, and the issue will be considered in more depth in Parts Three and Four. Whether or not poverty 'means' inequality, though, we need to recognise that on most of the tests, and in virtually every definition of poverty, inequality plays a part. People are poor, not just because of their own circumstances, but because of the circumstances of people around them. In any economic market, prices reflect a balance of supply and demand. When people have more resources to spend, prices go up. The best example is the price of land and housing. Housing and land prices depend mainly on the resources that other people have. If richer people have resources, and poorer people do not, the richer people can exclude the poorer people from housing. This happens in many places; rich people can afford second homes, while poor people live in unsatisfactory housing, and some have none at all. The principle works differently, however, for different commodities. Some prices, and conditions, are affected by the people around; others are not. This means that people might well be able to afford things which would be luxuries in other societies – like televisions or cameras – but might still be unable to afford essentials, like housing, transport or medical care. The implication of relative poverty, then, is that poverty is comparative – it has to be understood by comparing the position of people who are poor to those who are not poor.

The third meaning of 'relative poverty' is that the standard of poverty changes according to the society where it occurs. People in one country may be poor because they have no access to water or education; in another, where these are taken for granted, it may be because they do not have a warm, waterproof coat. Peter Townsend defines poverty in these terms:

> People are relatively deprived if they cannot obtain, at all, or sufficiently, the conditions of life – that is, the diets, amenities, standards and services which allow them to play the roles, participate in the relationships and follow the customary behaviour which is expected of them by virtue of their membership of society. If they lack or are denied the incomes, or more exactly the resources ... to obtain access to these conditions of life they can be defined to be in poverty.[18]

This goes further than either the social definition of poverty or the idea that inequality causes poverty. It identifies poverty in terms of what is accepted in a society. As society changes, so does the standard of poverty. The richer the society becomes, the higher that standard is likely to be.

In this sense, the idea of relative poverty is highly controversial. Townsend states that 'inequality is not poverty'[19], but his argument is not consistent with that: he defines poverty effectively as a form of disadvantage, and disadvantage is another name for inequality. People will be poor for as long as they are in a worse position than others.

Alternative approaches

A broader understanding of poverty has the effect of pointing to the similarities between different countries, as well as their differences. If we confine the meaning of poverty to income or physical resources, there may be little comparison between people in different countries; the contrast even within the countries of the EU makes direct comparison fairly meaningless. But many of the meanings of poverty cut across national and social divides. If poverty refers to inequality, then both rich and poor countries are unequal. If it refers to dependency, it happens in a wide range of countries. If it refers to social class, there are class divides everywhere.

The distinction between absolute and relative poverty has been emphasised less in recent years than it used to be. The *International Declaration*, referred to in Chapter One, states that:

> Absolute or basic material and social needs across societies are the same, even when they have to be satisfied differently according to institutions, culture and location.[20]

The key to understanding this lies in the phrase 'material and social needs'. Social relationships are as much part of poverty as material needs. The examples given in the *International Declaration* include the obligations of:

> parenthood, filial duties to the elderly, duties to friends, citizens and community and duties as workers to fellow workers and employers.

The ability to participate in society has to be understood in terms of social relationships, and in their nature such relationships depend on the society where they take place. Once we have started to understand social behaviour in these terms, the emphasis on material needs alone starts to look fairly inappropriate.

In *Voices of the poor*, the researchers identify ten interlocking dimensions of poverty:[21]

- *Precarious livelihoods.* The issue is not only that people lack the means of subsistence, but that there is a struggle to maintain their position – a state which is 'precarious'. Poor people have to manage as best they can; they are always vulnerable to change.
- *Excluded locations.* The position of areas and locations is partly a matter of physical geography, but it is also deeply affected by the social organisation of a community.
- *Physical health.* People's bodies, the researchers argue, are their principal asset. The problems of hunger, ill health, and exhaustion are a core part of the problems of poverty.
- *Gender relationships.* The issue of gender is fairly obviously about social relationships. In most societies, if not all, women are disadvantaged;

consequently, they are more likely to be vulnerable to poverty. Some writers have suggested that there has been a 'feminisation of poverty' in developed economies. The main reservation to make about this idea is that gender has always been a factor: there is nothing new about the disadvantage of women.[22]

- *Problems in social relationships.* A major element in poverty is the inability to participate in society.
- *Lack of security.* Insecurity is determined, not simply by lack of resources, but by the availability of protection – the ability to avoid harm when one is vulnerable.
- *Abuse by those in power.* For poor people, harassment by police and officials is part of the problem. In developed economies, the situation is much less aggrieved, though poor people and people in poor areas get a disproportionate amount of attention from the police.
- *Disempowering institutions.* This is a recurring theme, linked with the problem of abuse. In developed economies, government may be resented, but there is little doubt that it is supposed to act as a servant of the people. In many developing countries, the government in general, and the police in particular, may be part of the problem.
- *Weak community organisations.* The capacity of people to act with others depends on a set of structures and traditions, which tends to be weaker in poorer areas and poorer countries. It has become usual to talk about this capacity in terms of 'social capital'[23]; people can do more together than they can as individuals.
- *Limitations on the capabilities of the poor.* This is a very general theme, covering both the capacities of individuals and the capacity for collective and social action.

People are generally concerned with how they live and what they experience, more than they are with what they do not have. Many of these themes depend on social relationships more than material needs – on issues like relations with authority, gender, community organisation and the inability to participate in society.[24] In that respect, the issues that matter to poor people in developing countries are very much like the issues that matter to poor people in developed economies. Many issues are common to people in different cultures and different societies. Even if standards seem to differ, the problems of poverty do not.

THREE

Understanding the figures

Research into poverty

There are two main modes of social science research. 'Extensive' research tries to work out the scope and extent of the problem.[25] Typically, this kind of research is quantitative and normative. In poverty research, several researchers have developed a 'norm' or standard against which poverty can be judged, then use their research to determine whether or not poor people fall above or below the standard. Rowntree's pioneering research in York[26] used standards based on a normative household budget, and many researchers have followed similar approaches since then. Economic studies of the 'poverty line' are based on similar norms: researchers decide what level of income people ought to have, and find out how many people are below the line (the 'head count'), and by how much (the 'poverty gap'). In recent years, researchers have also developed an alternative approach, referred to as 'consensual' measures of poverty. The *Breadline Britain* surveys – another example of pioneering research done in the UK – began by finding out what people in the population thought of as essential – issues like inside toilets and enough beds for children – and then tried to establish who was unable to afford those standards.[27]

By contrast with extensive research, 'intensive' research goes into problems and processes, trying to work out what is happening.[28] Typically, intensive research is qualitative and descriptive. With regard to poverty, researchers go to areas and places where poor people live, and record what they see. They try to explain what poverty is like, and how it affects the people who experience it. The effect of combining research with arguments about policy has often been highly influential. The research helps to explain what the problems are, and how they might be understood; the arguments about policy suggest what might be done. The participatory studies of the World Bank, exemplified in *Voices of the poor*, have done much to shift the pattern of work in developing countries from an ideological view of economic reform through free markets, or 'structural adjustment', to approaches based in partnership and negotiation.

Research into poverty constantly falls foul of the moral elements in the idea of poverty. Debates that seem, at first sight, to be focused on concepts, methods and numbers are often moved by the sense that different results will have different implications for policy. Research matters, and the idea that it can be divorced from the values in the idea is unrealistic. Some years ago, David Piachaud wrote a stinging article about Peter Townsend's work, called 'Peter Townsend and the

Holy Grail'.[29] Townsend, Piachaud suggested, was attempting the impossible by trying to analyse poverty scientifically. Poverty is a normative (or value-laden) idea, and this shifts with the moral perspective of the person. Like the Holy Grail, this would always be out of the researcher's reach. This does not mean that scientific analysis is impossible; even if a concept is value-laden, it should still be possible to take it and analyse it scientifically. 'Health' is a similar kind of concept: people may take different views about what makes a person healthy, but that does not mean that it cannot be measured, assessed and improved. We need, though, to be aware that there are limits to how exact or precise it is possible to be. The limits rest, not in the process of research, but in the character of the idea that is being examined.

Measuring poverty

Because poverty means lots of things, it is difficult to measure. It is possible to measure issues like income, inequality or deprivation, but that is not the same as measuring poverty as a whole. It may be possible to look at the elements of poverty separately, measuring the factors one by one, giving special emphasis to circumstances where these factors overlap. Alternatively, patterns of poverty can be deciphered and interpreted from a range of information. This is generally done in terms of 'social indicators'.

A social indicator can be seen as:

> a statistic of direct normative interest facilitating concise, comprehensive and balanced judgment about the condition of major aspects of society.[30]

The term 'indicator' means what it says, and it was chosen for that reason.[31] An indicator is a signpost or pointer. It is a way of representing something, not necessarily the thing itself. One thing can point to another. The unemployment rate is an indicator of economic activity; a child's weight is an indicator of developmental progress; premature mortality is an indicator of ill health. None of these is a measure; we cannot tell that people are in good health just because they have not died. But we can say that, where many people die young, the population as a whole is almost certainly not in good health. Box 3 gives some illustrative indicators on poverty.

There are many reasons for producing indicators. Agencies want useful information. They do not necessarily want the information to be exactly right, because precise measurement cannot be matched by precise policy responses, but they want information which is valid – that is, information which will relate to the issues. They want to apply information which is available, because new information can be expensive to generate. And they want sufficient information to work out what they have done, and what effect their policies have. Often the data on social issues are unreliable. This is particularly true in developing countries, where surveys are difficult to mount and data are often incomplete, unreliable and difficult to replicate. Many of the figures used by the UNDP for the Human Development Index are invented to fill in the gaps: they assume that missing values are worth 25%, on the basis that a country which is unable to say even approximately whether its people have access to water or education probably has a sizeable shortfall.[32] Contrast a widely used, and much criticised, indicator: the World Bank estimates 'poverty' as happening when people's income is a dollar or two dollars a day. The indicator is criticised in no less than six chapters of Townsend and Gordon's edited collection on *World poverty*.[33] Understood as a measure, a dollar a day cannot be defended. Poverty cannot be summed up in a single measure; the standard is way too low; income is not enough; it is not really possible to say what a dollar a day means in many societies; and the standard is not genuinely comparable. But the criticisms miss the point. A dollar a day fits the tests for indicators. It may not be accurate, but it is useful. It is easy to understand, accessible and cheap. It gives some idea of whether problems are getting better or worse. It works as a signpost.

Measures can be indicators, and indicators can be measures. Like a good measure, a good indicator will follow the pattern of the thing it indicates: if income is an indicator of poverty, it should go up when poverty goes down, and it should go down when poverty goes up. A good measure reflects the nature of the thing it is measuring, and it ought to be accurate. A good indicator makes people aware of the issues it is indicating, and, because it is supposed to reflect the characteristics of the problems it identified, it ought to have a consistent relationship with it. These aims are clearly compatible, but they are difficult to achieve, and sometimes one has to be sacrificed for another. Good measures can be bad indicators. For example, criminal convictions are more precise than reported crime, and reported crime is more precise than survey reports on crime, but in each case the less precise figure is more meaningful. Conversely, good indicators can be bad measures: no one should imagine that poverty is measurable in terms of income, low birthweight or housing tenure, but they are useful pointers to the issues.

Presenting indicators

There are three main ways of presenting indicators: headline indicators, summary indices and multiple indicators.

Headline indicators. A 'headline' indicator is a single figure, giving a simple, selective view. Commonly used examples are the use of income inequality as an indicator of poverty, infant mortality as an indicator of general health in developing countries, or the growth rate as a proxy for economic development. None of these describes the issues fully and precisely, but they serve, and even if there are

Box 3: Human development – indicators of poverty

The Human Development Index (HDI) is produced by the UNDP. It ranks countries by a range of factors, including:

- longevity, as an indicator of health
- education
- a decent standard of living, mainly measured by GDP per capita and income inequality
- gender inequality and
- in developed economies, long-term unemployment (as an indicator of social exclusion).

Table 3.1 presents a few figures taken from the UNDP's statistics for relatively developed economies.[34] There are many problems with the statistics, and as countries become poorer, the figures become progressively less and less reliable.

Table 3.1: Indicators of poverty

Country	GDP per capita, 2002 ($)	Probability of death under age 60 (%)	People lacking functional literacy skills (%)	Long-term unemploy-ment (%)	Relative income poverty (% under 50% of median income)	Index of gender equality (1.0 would be equal)
Netherlands	29,100	8.7	10.5	0.8	7.3	0.938
UK	26,150	8.9	21.8	1.2	12.5	0.934
US	35,750	12.6	20.7	0.5	17	0.936
France	26,920	10	na	3	8	0.929
Poland	10,560	15.6	42.6	9.6	8.6	0.848
Russia	8,230	28.9	na	na	18.8	0.794

Taken across all countries, the UNDP figures show that:

- Although richer countries generally have fewer problems than poorer ones, there is considerable variation as to which are better at avoiding the problems of poverty. The US does noticeably worse on many indicators than many European nations with lower incomes.
- Doing well in one respect does not necessarily mean that a country does well in others. Some countries in the process of development are much more unequal than others.
- There are considerable problems in many nations. Nearly half the population of Portugal lacks basic literacy skills. Hungary is markedly richer than Poland (GDP per capita is $13,400 a year), but nearly a fifth of its population dies before the age of 60. 18% of the population of Turkey, which is a candidate for membership of the EU, do not have access to clean water.

exceptions they can be defended in broad terms. The argument for headline indicators is, more or less, that if a headline indicator is not devised expressly, one will be used anyway. The EU uses a basic income measure, which is used across the EU because nothing else does as well.

What makes a good headline indicator? First, the indicator has to be available and (at least apparently) comprehensible. Second, it has to have a fairly general application, pointing to more than it appears. Infant mortality is strongly associated with adult health, economic growth with welfare, and income with command over resources. (There are obvious exceptions: for example, in some circumstances economic growth can imply reduced welfare.) Third, measures to improve the headline indicator should have associated benefits in other areas. A high rate of infant mortality is usually indicative of poor nutrition coupled with infective and parasitic diseases. Measures which address those issues have a much wider implication for health.

Most headline indicators of poverty are related to income. Income is a valuable indicator, for several reasons. It is relatively easily measurable. It is strongly associated with many other indicators of welfare. Increased income is usually indicative of increased welfare, though once again this is not necessarily true: in developing countries, a child who leaves school to sell things in the street will have a higher income, and will add to GDP, but this is suggestive of lower welfare. In the same vein, *The Economist* points out that 'a disease that kills millions of children and old people can produce a rise in GDP per head if those aged 15-45, the most economically productive members of society, are still standing but there are fewer people in total to share the wealth'.[35] The main problem with the use of income as a headline indicator has been the tendency for the focus on income to drive out other forms of discussion. Many commentators, especially in the US, make no distinction between concepts of poverty and income thresholds.

Summary indices. The second option is to use a summary index. A summary index consists of a set of indicators which are compiled in order to produce a composite measure. An example is the HDI described in Box 3. There are some general points which need to be considered:

- *Validity.* Indices have to measure what they are supposed to measure, and cross-validation is difficult. An index can be cross-validated with issues which are not part of it, like income or benefit receipt, or by the association of items within the index itself. The items should be correlated with each other – but not too highly, because a very strong association suggests that the same issue is being counted twice. This is a matter of judgement. Even then, with a multidimensional set of issues like poverty, there is the problem that indicators may not fully reflect the range of issues which are of concern. In the measurement of child poverty, for example, major issues affecting large numbers of people, like income, poor health and social exclusion, may dwarf smaller numbers in critical problem areas, like school exclusions or serious unintentional injury.

- *Reliability.* Indices which are reliable within a particular social context, or at a certain period, are not necessarily transferable to other circumstances. Measures of poverty or inflation based on a 'basket of goods' depend crucially on what the goods are.
- *Quantification.* The construction of indices assumes linear mathematical relationships. Some of the problems in indices of poverty, like gender equality and access to water, cannot simply be added together.
- *Inclusion and exclusion of relevant factors.* Exclusions lead to important issues being ignored: housing standards, for example, now rarely feature in indices of deprivation. Over-inclusion can lead to greater weight being given to particular factors: for example, in some countries the definition of 'disability' reflects people's ability to work, so that changes in the labour market are double-counted when both unemployment and disability are included in indices.
- *Weighting.* Factors have to be given appropriate weights, which depends partly on appropriate quantification, and partly on normative judgement. All weighting, including that made through statistical analysis or taking averages, implicitly reflects some kind of value judgement.
- *Norms and values.* In some cases, the norms and values contained in summary indices will be evident: it is difficult to present material on human rights, for example, without a fairly explicit statement of value. However, because summary indices tend to conceal their constituent elements, they also tend to conceal the norms and values implicit in the constituent judgements. Some of these effects are indirect: for example, the implication of emphasising long-term unemployment is often to emphasise the disadvantage experienced by men, who are more likely to be counted in those figures than women. Some are direct: the choices of inclusion, exclusions and weighting have an immediate effect on the relationships identified through such indices.

Multiple indicators. The third approach is to retain several dimensions of indicators. An example is the use of indicators in the UK government series *Opportunity for all.*[36] The indicators for children and young people, as an example, are these:

Improving family incomes	• children in workless households
	• low income (three indicators)
Early years and education	• Key Stage 1 attainment (7–year-olds)
	• Key Stage 2 attainment (11–year-olds)
	• 16–year-olds with one GCSE
	• 19–year-olds with level 2 qualification
	• truancies
	• school exclusion

	• attainment of children looked after by local authorities
Quality of life	• housing conditions • infant mortality • smoking rates (pregnant women and children aged 11–15) • serious unintentional injury • re-registrations on Child Protection Register
Transition to adult life	• teenage conceptions • teenage parents not in education, employment or training • 16- to 18-year-olds in education.

There are three main arguments for using multiple indicators. The first is methodological. Issues that are difficult to identify or research are generally focused on by 'triangulation' – approaching the problems in several different ways. Researchers into attitudes, for example, do not waste their time looking for a single question that captures every shade of attitude: they ask questions in bundles, so that they can cross-reference the answer. In the same way, multiple indicators are used for cross-confirmation: the more frequently an issue is identified, the more likely it is that something is there. If indicators are concerned with complex problems, multiple indicators help to examine a problem from different perspectives.

The second argument is practical. Multiple indicators offer more detailed, disaggregated information. Local and voluntary agencies engaged in policy making are often required to provide baseline information and indicators as evidence of their effectiveness; the more detail that is made available to them, the better able they are to respond. That is the source of the demand for neighbourhood statistics, which have made current indicators available at a detailed local level. The same argument applies at every level of the policy-making process.

Third, there is an argument from principle. When dealing with complex, multidimensional issues, the effect of aggregating and simplifying is to reduce the complexity at the expense of minor issues, which are overridden by weightier ones. Whether this matters depends on importance attached to those issues. Poverty has many faces, but they have something in common: they all make a normative claim for attention. If a concept like 'poverty' is treated as a whole, specific, important factors which only relate to a part of the problem – like gender inequalities, homelessness, or educational attainment – are likely to be outweighed or ignored. The main disadvantage of using multiple indicators is that they are complex, and may be too complex to be digested easily.

The analysis of poverty

This has been a brief skate over a vast field. There are certain lessons to draw from it. The first is that we need to be very, very sceptical about a lot of the figures and research which are presented about poverty. They do not mean what they say. The second is that, despite this scepticism, we need to be tolerant about the figures. Many of the most useful ones, like income, low birthweight, early death or employment, are measuring something different from poverty. They are still useful, nevertheless, because they point us towards the kinds of issue we need to know about – issues such as people's needs, their resources, or their social situation. According to the World Bank, half of the world's population lives on less than two dollars a day. This may not be the most meaningful of statements, but it points, however vaguely, to something that matters a great deal. The figures are presented in Table 3.2.[37]

Table 3.2: World Bank figures on global poverty

	Millions		% of the world's population	
	1990	2001	1990	2001
Below $1 a day	1,219	1,101	27.9	21.3
Below $2 a day	2,689	2,733	61.6	52.8

Part Two
Poverty as material need

FOUR

Concepts of need

Understood in terms of material need, poverty covers many issues. Chapter One outlined three main clusters of meaning: poverty as deprivation, poverty as a pattern of deprivation and poverty as a low standard of living. This is only one way of breaking down the issues, and there are many possible sub-divisions. The ideas of 'absolute' and 'relative' poverty discussed in Chapter Two can both be seen as ways of discussing material need, and concepts like 'basic needs' or 'relative deprivation' involve an elaborate framework of ideas underpinning a basic understanding of poverty as the lack of something.

The idea of need

'Needs' have two elements. In the first instance, needs are problems. Needs occur in circumstances where a person is likely to experience something bad, or suffer harm. We sometimes talk loosely about conditions like illness, disability and old age as 'needs' on that basis; the 'assessment of needs' undertaken when governments compare poor areas is little more than a comparison of problems. Second, a need requires a response. It is not enough to say that harm is going to happen; there has to be some way of reducing the harm, or preventing it. Malnutrition is a need for food; homelessness is a need for shelter; illness is commonly taken to require medical intervention. At times, the response is taken to be so obvious that responses to problems are described as 'needs' in themselves. It is not unusual to hear the claim that 'this area needs more nurses' or that 'these people need counselling'. Strictly speaking, a response is hardly ever directly justified only by identification of a problem. Problems can be addressed in many ways: there are several options besides nursing to give medical support or domiciliary care, and there are other options besides counselling available to deal with emotional trauma or distress. The available responses, and the resources we have to provide them, are likely to affect the interpretation of the problem.

Because all needs require a response, the statement that someone is in need is always, in some sense, a claim – a demand for a response. Arguments about famine, homelessness or fuel poverty are, clearly, claims for food, for shelter and for warmth. The kinds of claim people are ready to make depend on the kinds of responses that are available. We may be content to accept that someone who is suffering from a parasitic disease needs medical treatment, because most parasitic diseases are capable of being treated. We are much less likely to say that someone with a respiratory disease needs air conditioning, because although air conditioning is a possible response, and it may help with the problem, in most countries it is neither accessible nor affordable.

Saying that poverty is a form of material need has, then, some fairly direct implications. It says that people in poverty have problems. It says that a response is available. And it says, as has been pointed out before, that something ought to be done about it. For some readers, this will all seem so obvious that it is not worth saying, but it is worth stressing the point for others who take a different view of poverty. An understanding of poverty based on need is not about being on a low income, or having fewer opportunities, or even 'going without'; it is a situation where people are suffering (see Box 4).

Box 4: Malnutrition

Malnutrition is mainly identified by looking at measurements of height and weight. The three main indicators are:
- underweight – being a low weight for one's age
- wasting – being underweight for one's height and
- stunting – being a low height for one's age.

Stunting is the most prevalent problem, affecting about a third of children in developing countries.

Table 4.1 presents figures for the three indicators from the UNICEF database.[38] Figures are not kept for most industrial countries, where the problems are generally not significant; the main exception is the US, where some people are malnourished despite the country's wealth.

Table 4.1: Percentage of children under five years of age with moderate and severe malnutrition in selected countries

Country	Underweight	Wasting	Stunting
US	1	1	2
Hungary	2	2	3
Russia	3	4	13
Brazil	6	2	11
China	8	na	14
India	47	16	46
Ethiopia	47	11	52

Malnutrition is not just a claim for people to be fed. Only 'wasting' directly demonstrates an immediate need for food at the time when the statistic is compiled. Stunting and underweight are indicators of a history of malnutrition. They chart the implications of malnutrition for physical development over time. They are, then, pointers to a more widespread, underlying problem. The claim they help to establish is a general claim for improvement in the distribution of food resources, not just the relief of hunger.

Material needs

People have many different needs, and the idea of poverty is not concerned with all of them. People have physical needs, like nutrition, health and sexual relations. They have psychological needs, like needs for nurture, personal development and emotional expression and attachment. They have social needs, like family relationships, friendship and company, opportunity and social respect. The focus on 'material need' cuts across many others, and it does not include everything that might be considered to be part of poverty, because there are also views of poverty which focus on social needs. Material needs are needs which require material resources – goods, commodities and services – to be satisfied. There is a strong element of social convention in this. Housing, food and medical care are bought and sold; friendship, company and personal relationships are not. Poverty is concerned, because of this, with the former group, not the latter. (The distinction is not clear cut: normal family relationships make housing and food available outside the market, and people need money to keep social contact with friends.)

The discussion of absolute and relative poverty in Chapter Two points to the kinds of material need which people have to satisfy. In general terms, these needs may be common across cultures, but they are also socially constructed. The *Breadline Britain* surveys established a method for identifying the kinds of thing that people thought were socially necessary. The figures in Table 4.2 show the results of three different surveys, in 1983, 1990 and 1999. More than 90% of respondents in all three surveys thought that people needed heat, a home free from damp, and beds for everyone. It is difficult not to be swayed by the number of people thinking that inside toilets and refrigerators are necessary, though both standards seem to have developed only since the 1950s. The standards are not so obvious they can be taken for granted. Pre-war housing had ventilated food cupboards rather than refrigerators, and some people thought that inside toilets were unhygienic. More than that, the standards are strongly relative to culture; for example, the British horror of children sharing beds is not universal. In a survey in a Mexican town, the respondents included aftershave and dental floss in the list of essentials.[39] The inclusion of aftershave is surprising, because an item which is only used by clean-shaven adult males does not seem likely to command extensive support across the population, but the point helps to emphasise the importance of cultural norms in deciding what is, and what is not, essential.

Needs and resources

The idea of need involves both problems and the resources to meet them, and understood in this way, the same applies to poverty. Material need involves, on one hand, material deprivation: the lack of the things that people have to have to avoid harm. These are things like food, clothing, fuel and shelter. They involve

Table 4.2: 'Necessities'

	Thinking necessary (%)			Unable to afford (%)		
	1983	1990	1999	1983	1990	1999
Housing						
Heating	97	97	94	5	3	1
Indoor toilet	96	97	–	2	0	–
Damp-free home	96	98	93	7	2	6
Bath	94	95	–	2	0	–
Decent home decoration	–	92	82	–	15	14
Enough bedrooms for children	77	82	–	3	7	–
Food						
Two meals a day for adults	64	90	91	3	1	1
Three meals a day for children	82	90	–	2	0	–
Fresh fruit and vegetables daily	–	88	86	–	6	4
Meat or equivalent every other day	63	77	79	8	4	3
Clothing						
Warm waterproof coat	87	91	85	7	4	4
Two pairs of all-weather shoes	78	74	64	9	5	5
Household goods						
Beds for everyone	94	95	95	1	1	1
Repair or replace electrical goods	–	–	85	–	–	12
Refrigerator	77	92	89	2	1	0
Carpets	70	78	67	2	2	3
Washing machine	67	73	76	6	4	1
Financial security						
Insurance	–	88	79	–	10	8
Savings of £10 per month	–	68	66	–	30	25
Quality of life						
Visits to friends or family	–	–	84	–	–	2
Toys for children	71	84	–	2	2	–
Celebrations	69	74	83	4	4	2
Presents once a year	63	69	56	5	5	3
Hobby or leisure activity	64	67	78	7	7	7

Sources: J Mack and S Lansley, 1985, *Poor Britain*, London: Allen and Unwin; D Gordon and C Pantazis (eds) 1996, *Breadline Britain in the 1990s*, London: Avebury; D Gordon, L Adelman, K Ashworth, J Bradshaw, R Levitas, S Middleton, C Pantazis, D Patisos, S Payne, P Townsend and J Williams, 1999, *Poverty and social exclusion in Britain*, York: Joseph Rowntree Foundation

services like medical care, transport and education. Material need also implies, though, a need for resources to obtain these things. Resources are conventionally understood in terms of income and wealth, but in fact the kinds of resources which matter go well beyond this. People's needs may be met through a variety of other routes, including support from family and friends, communal activity and state provision. If an older person with limited physical capability needs help with domestic chores, it can be done by a husband or wife (the main source of personal care); a family member, like a son, daughter, or daughter-in-law (the gender bias in this reflects the main form of such relationships); a neighbour or friend; provision by the state; or by paying for domestic help. When people's 'needs' are assessed, they tend to be interpreted in terms of the resources available. When we say that people are lacking resources, we usually mean not that they are short of money, but that they are short of money after their other resources have been taken into account.

People meet their needs, in general, by using their resources. If they are short of resources, then either their needs will not be satisfied, or they will have to meet them by trying to use resources in a different way. Very few people have no resources at all – a condition we refer to as 'destitution' rather than poverty. Poor people are mainly people who do not have enough resources, rather than people who have none. This means that, typically, poverty is not just about going without things. People who lack resources have to manage as best they can. They go without food one day to have fuel the next. They go without fuel to get health care for their children; and so it goes on. One of the central problems of research into poverty is that it is trying to describe a moving target.

Deprivation

Deprivation means, in the first instance, that someone is lacking something. Brown and Madge write:

> Deprivations are loosely regarded as unsatisfactory and undesirable circumstances, whether material, emotional, physical or behavioural, as recognised by a fair degree of societal consensus. Deprivations involve a lack of something generally held to be desirable – an adequate income, good health, etc – a lack which is associated to a greater or lesser extent with some degree of suffering.[40]

This comes very close to the definition of 'need' given earlier, though it is more narrowly understood. People can have needs which are satisfied. Deprivation is what happens when their needs are not met.

There is, however, another understanding of 'deprivation', one that takes it away from the focus on suffering or harm. Peter Townsend defines deprivation in terms of disadvantage:

> Deprivation may be defined as a state of observable and demonstrable disadvantage relative to the local community or the wider society or nation to which an individual, family or group belongs.[41]

People can be disadvantaged if they are in a less desirable position than others. That does not necessarily mean that they are suffering harm; it might be that they do not have the access to privileges or luxuries that other people have. In a society like Britain, where most people have a colour television, a tumble dryer and access to the Internet, the implication of Townsend's definition is that people who do not can be said to be 'deprived'. Townsend is an influential writer, and many people have been persuaded by his arguments, but I do not think this is how most of us understand the term. People are 'deprived' when they lack something they need. This means that they are suffering some kind of harm, and so that they are lacking welfare.

The link between poverty and deprivation is strong, because many senses of 'poverty' are concerned with lack of welfare, hardship and material need. People can be deprived without being poor, because lacking a specific need – for example, a bed for each child, or insurance against loss – might come to something less than poverty. Similarly, a short-term need – like missing food while waiting for a first pay cheque – might not be thought of as amounting to poverty, though it is clearly a form of deprivation. There are not many senses of poverty, however, which do not involve deprivation in some form, either because poverty is defined as deprivation, or because poverty is a cause of deprivation.

Patterns of deprivation

One of the conventional ways in which poverty has been described is as a low standard of living. Because poor people have limited resources, they generally have less access to the goods, amenities and services that other people have. The standard of living is usually measured in terms of poor people's consumption, or indirectly through looking at their resources – mainly their income. The International Labour Organization, for example, suggests that

> At the simplest level, individuals or families are considered poor when their level of living, measured in terms of income or consumption, is below a particular standard.[42]

This is why research into poverty looks at issues like household budgets (Rowntree's research referred to the 'standard of life'). Household budgets are a way of working out what people consume. Budgets are useful, because they offer a way of trying to understand how poor people balance their needs with their resources. Their main weakness is that, in their nature, they tend to focus on the things that are consumed regularly (like food and fuel) and miss the slow, gradual wear and tear on furnishings and housing which lead over time to large expenditures when items have to be replaced.

People's standard of living is closely linked to their needs, but it is not the same as needs. The shift from considering needs to a standard of living starts to take into account the things that people do not need, as well as those they do. Rowntree's standard of 'primary poverty' used a very strict test of what people needed: he did not allow for tea, newspapers or transport. If we are thinking about people's 'standard of living' instead, it goes beyond the strict essentials, to take into account much more general information about their lifestyle. People can bear some needs without necessarily depriving themselves of things which may seem to be less essential. For example, people might go without food to pay for cigarettes.

One understanding of poverty is that it represents the circumstances not only of those people who *are* in need but also of those whose position means they *might* be. Charles Booth wrote of poor people as 'living under a struggle to obtain the necessaries of life and make both ends met'.[43] Poor people are not just people in need. They include people who are on the margins – people who are trying not to be in need, people who are insecure, and people who are vulnerable to need. Poor people are likely to be vulnerable, but vulnerability and insecurity are not the same thing as poverty; they apply to many people who are not poor, and there are circumstances where richer people are more vulnerable than poor ones. The distinction is particularly important in developing countries, where the effect of economic development may also be to increase vulnerability.

> Diversified subsistence farmers may be poor but are not vulnerable. When they enter the market by selling specialised cash crops, or raising their earnings by incurring debts, or investing in risky ventures, their incomes rise, but they become vulnerable. There are trade-offs between poverty and vulnerability (or between security and income).[44]

Putting this another way, people may have a higher standard of living but be less secure.

The idea of a 'standard of living' tends to assume some consistency in the lifestyles of poor people. This may not be true. Because poverty changes constantly, it is often described in terms of the pattern of deprivation, rather than the type of deprivation. We cannot say for certain that because someone is homeless, that person must be poor. People can be homeless for many reasons – for example, fire, flood or natural disaster. We can tell that homelessness is the result of poverty when it is part of a pattern of poverty. This manifests itself in two main forms. The first is that people can experience, not one type of deprivation, but several. The more types of deprivation a person experiences, and the more often it happens, the more likely it is that the person is poor. The research for *Breadline Britain* initially suggested that people were poor if they suffered from three main types of deprivation.[45] There is no clear threshold or cut-off point which makes it possible to say this with any certainty.[46] Finding three types of deprivation raises at least the plausible suspicion that the deprivations are not coincidental, and that there is an underlying set of problems. (Later research, using the same basic methods, reduced the number of factors to two, which is less convincing.[47]) The argument depends on the assumption that problems which occur together might reflect a common cause, or at least an underlying set of issues. Where there is poverty, there will be more than one problem, and even if we cannot say what the problems will be, we know that poverty will typically generate a few of them. This is not quite the same thing as saying that poverty is multiple deprivation, because there is no clear pattern of deprivation implied by it; but because the problems of poverty rarely come separately, it comes close.

The second view is more subtle, and more difficult to identify in a survey. It is expressed in the idea that there is a 'web' of deprivation. The writers who coined the idea[48] were trying to come to terms with a practical problem in their research, that none of the families they wanted to study met their predetermined criteria. What they found, in place of those criteria, was constant change and shifting circumstances. But that did not necessarily mean that people were moving out of poverty. What happened, rather, was that people seemed to get out of one set of problems only to get into others. The idea of the 'web' of deprivation is drawn from the efforts of a fly to escape from a spider's web: lifting up one limb is possible if another presses down, and the fly cannot free enough limbs to escape. The image of the web is a persuasive one. Unlike the idea of multiple deprivation, it does not suppose that there is an identifiable pattern or constellation of problems that will occur together predictably. The difficulty with it is that it makes it impossible to be precise: if poverty is constantly shifting and changing, and people never have quite the same problems, how can we identify and measure it? Equally, if people escape from some problems only to fall into others, it offers politicians the unappealing prospect of dealing with a set of wicked, intractable problems where it is difficult to see how effective policies have been. The idea of a web of deprivation makes sense, and it may just be right. In the real world, unfortunately, that is not good enough.

FIVE

Area deprivation

Poverty and poor areas

For over a century, social scientists have understood the concept of poverty principally as a property of individuals, families or households. Poverty is not usually referred to as an attribute of groups, communities or regions. The concept of poverty has been individualised; the 'poverty' of poor areas is simply a figure lumping together the conditions of the people who live in them.

On this basis, the proposition that areas can be poor is questionable. There are higher concentrations in the poorest areas of different kinds of social problem, but poverty is widely dispersed; most poor people do not live in poor areas. In developing countries, there are concentrations of relatively bad housing (see Box 5), but they are still home to a minority of the poor. In developed economies, it is also true that most poor people do not live in poor areas; but beyond that, most of the people living in poor areas are not poor. The Social Exclusion Unit's figures on the 'worst' areas in Britain show some concentration of problems, with 44 districts having 85% of the most deprived electoral wards. Their report does not, however, show that most people in the worst areas were deprived. Less than half the children in these areas live in families on low incomes; only 20% of the population were unemployed, and less than 10% were single parents.[49] The basic objection to describing the 'areas' as poor is, simply, that it misrepresents the situation of the people who live there.

The claim that such areas are poor nevertheless can be understood in two senses. The first is the argument that there is something about these areas which helps to explain the greater vulnerability to poverty of the people who live in them. The second, stronger sense is that the area itself is poor, even if many of the people in it are not.

The reasons why an area is thought of as 'desirable' or 'undesirable' may not have anything to do with poverty. Design, location, proximity to facilities and environmental factors may influence people's choices; but other factors, like population density, maintenance and the history of the area come into play, shaping the way the area is perceived and directing the pattern of future occupancy. Once areas are identified as more or less desirable – that is, sought after by more people, and people who are prepared to pay more – economic status plays a major part in determining who is going to live there. It happens, in part, that people who have the resources to move to more desirable places are able to do so; this process is described by William Julius Wilson.[50] It may also be true that there is a process of selection, which excludes poor people from more desirable areas and pushes them towards less desirable ones. Even in public housing, poor people are brought together by their inability to choose. The least desirable housing tends to go to people on lower incomes, living in worse conditions; the more sought–after housing goes to people on higher incomes, living in better conditions, who are better able to wait until they get what they want.[51]

When there are problems in an area, poverty can make them worse. In part, this happens because poor people are likely to be people with other problems: they may be poor because they are unemployed, have mental health problems, are single parents or have low educational attainment. These are not only people with low resources; they are often stigmatised and excluded. Concentrating poor people in particular places means that there is also a concentration of this

Box 5: Slums

More than a billion people, worldwide, live in slums. UN-Habitat uses five factors to define a slum: lack of any one of them is enough. The factors are:
- access to safe water
- access to sanitation
- secure tenure
- durability of housing and
- sufficient living area.

Estimates for 2005 are given in Table 5.1.[53]

Table 5.1: Slum dwellers

Region	Number of people in slums (2005 estimates)
Europe	33,368,000
Other developed countries	21,903,000
North Africa	21,224,000
Sub-Saharan Africa	199,231,000
Latin America and the Caribbean	134,257,000
East Asia	212,368,000
South and Central Asia	285,713,000
South East Asia	59,913,000
Western Asia	46,709,000
Oceania	568,000
Total	**1,015,254,000**

Slums are not just a question of bad housing. They are also *concentrations* of bad housing – locations where bad housing is found next to other bad housing. Access to land, housing and facilities all depend on people's financial resources. Where people live depends on their ability to choose.

kind of issue, and the place itself develops a bad reputation. It also happens that poverty and a lack of resources lead to other problems in the places where poverty occurs. Areal factors like housing and the environment may cause poor health.[52] Poverty is associated with poor housing conditions, not just because poor people have to live in bad housing, but because their poverty makes the conditions worse; lack of resources may mean problems of heating, dampness, and lack of maintenance and poor commercial facilities in the immediate locality. In some cases, property which is adequately designed for better-off tenants has proved to be inadequate for poorer people: high-rise buildings, which have been successful for some groups, are associated with isolation, poor maintenance and a lack of play space. The problems of living in a bad area are greater when one is poor.

Do areas cause poverty?

The idea that areas 'cause' poverty can be taken in two ways. In the weaker sense, areas 'cause' poverty if they take poverty and make it worse. In the stronger sense, they cause poverty if they make people poor. There are four main accounts of the process by which areas might cause poverty:

1   *Environmental determinism.* Some writers have argued that space, location and territory have an effect independent of economic factors.[54] Industrially built housing has been associated with structural defects, inadequate estate design, faults in the internal design of dwellings, and noise; these problems are often associated with social problems. The work that makes these claims has defects; there are problems both in the kinds of indicators used to identify the prevalence of social problems, and the attempt to interpret these factors in terms of design.[55] There may, however, be effects which result from the interaction of the poverty of the tenants and the design of estates.

2   *The effects of an area on social relationships.* The literature on this subject has always been controversial. The core of the argument is the proposition that being close to other poor people generates patterns of social contact, which in turn lead to identifiably different patterns of behaviour. Some commentators have considered the impact of neighbourhood on the levels of teenage pregnancy.[56] Anderson attributes the pattern of behaviour to sub-cultural influences, peer group influence and 'role models'.

3   *Area-based resources.* The implication of a process in which there are greater concentrations of poor people in some areas than others – whether or not these concentrations amount to a considerable majority of people – is that the economic resources in these areas are different from those elsewhere. First, facilities in the area which depend on economic participation or disposable income – like shops, post offices or pharmacies – are less likely to survive. Second, living in particular areas has a direct effect on the

services which one receives: middle-class areas tend to have a greater resource base and lower needs. Third, the reputation of an area may also have an effect on its resources. People who live in 'bad areas' may find it difficult to get credit, insurance premiums may be higher, and residents may not be able to get commercial deliveries or transport services.

4   *Spatial determinants of employment and the labour market.* The conditions which most obviously produce poverty – the structure of the economy, and the pattern of employment – have a strong spatial dimension. Cities have developed, historically, with a mix of residential, industrial and commercial facilities. Geographically, the implications of this development is not to create a random mix, but rather differing areal locations for different activities, often reinforced by planning restrictions. It also happens that living near higher numbers of people who are unemployed affects job prospects in itself. The process is straightforward enough – where jobs become available which are accessible, there will be more competition at similar levels of skill. Residence in a particular area is likely, then, to be associated with employment prospects. Under these circumstances, it is not surprising that certain areas of cities have tended be associated with higher levels of employment than others; indeed, it would have been astonishing if they were not.

Areas make poverty worse. Certain resources are based on particular locations, and that must mean that location directly affects command over resources. But beyond that, do areas create or generate poverty? People who live in particular areas are more likely than people in other areas to be poor as a consequence of the place where they live. The processes by which this can come about are clear, and the answer has to be 'yes'.

Are areas poor?

Some writers have objected to the idea that an area can be poor.[57] The central objection is individualistic: that there is no such thing as an area, only the people who make it up. It is not, then, areas which have problems or low incomes, but the people who live in them. It would still follow that the area will have a higher concentration of poor people than elsewhere; it will have a variety of social problems; and the conditions of poor people are likely to be worse than if the same people lived elsewhere. Even from an individualistic perspective, then, there is still a case for considering the impact of location on poverty.

The case for shifting the focus of attention to the area becomes markedly stronger when attention moves to people who are not themselves poor. Living in a poor area can make them worse off. It happens, for example, through the lack of community resources, the increased competition for places in the labour market, and the effect of stigmatisation on command over resources. Further, people who live in such areas are less secure than others. The fear of crime is directly associated with perceptions of the physical deterioration of an area,[58] but the problems are not simply a matter of perception. People who are on higher incomes in lower-income areas have greater vulnerability to crime than people elsewhere, including burglary, robbery, motor vehicle theft and vandalism.[59] These people are not likely to be made poor in consequence – that would happen only if the effect of living in the area was to bring their level of resources down enough for them to be considered as deprived – but anyone in this position has lower resources, other things being equal, than others who have desirable, well-maintained environments.

This is a crucial point. What the findings about non-poor people show is that the problems of poor areas cannot be reduced to problems of poor people within those areas. The issues are related to the problems of poor individuals and families, but they are not always the same problems.

This argument still starts from the premise that the poverty of an area can be understood in individual terms. If the idea of poverty is not confined to individuals – and there seems to be no good reason that it should be – there is no difficulty in applying the concept to areas and neighbourhoods as collective social units. Although poor areas are likely to have more poor people than other areas, they are not simply defined by the relative numbers of poor people. Poor areas are identifiable in terms of their characteristics as areas: they have poor housing, a run-down environment, a lack of security and low status. The environment, the economic base, the social status of the area and the infrastructure of services are developed at an area level. The question to ask is not just whether individuals are poor, but whether areas are. There is a constellation of inter-related deprivations which has to be understood at the level of the area. It follows that there *is* such a thing as a poor area.

How we lost sight of area poverty

The argument of this chapter largely squares with 'common sense' – or popular prejudice. Social scientists often take a delight in showing that common sense is wrong, not least because findings which run counter to popular prejudice do much to justify their existence. In this case, however, it may be the social scientists who have it wrong.

The process began with Charles Booth's initial research into poverty in Victorian London. Starting in the 1880s, he undertook a massive research project, identifying and describing the living conditions of poor people throughout London.[60] The research undertaken by Booth's team was mainly qualitative and descriptive; his researchers visited the houses and places of work of poor people; they went to schools and institutions; they took evidence from expert witnesses. Much of this work is forgotten now, though it pioneered methods that have become the staple of social research since. Booth was strongly aware of the importance of problems in areas – he went so far as to chart the distribution of poverty and the character of different neighbourhoods. The issue he identified was not simply that there was a spatial dimension to poverty – Booth refers to some areas as 'poverty traps' – but that the housing and environment of the poor were no less issues.[61] The debate which followed Booth's initial work, however, concentrated on a particular aspect of the research – the idea of a 'poverty line', a term which Booth invented, and his use of household budgets. For Booth, the 'poverty line' was not a threshold, but a range of income – roughly the wage of the lowest-paid full-time workers – below which people were likely to be poor. Booth used household budgets only as a supplement to other information about poverty, and that for only a small number of indicative cases; but because these were the focus of public criticism, they also became the main focus for further research. Rowntree's subsequent research in York used the idea of household budgets, and his measurement of poverty was based principally in the income available to households.[62] The study of poverty was subsequently defined in terms of household income – to the point where other aspects of the experience of limited resources were obscured. The meaning of 'poverty' in social research effectively changed, from a general concern with problems associated with low resources to those of limited incomes. It remained the dominant focus during the 'rediscovery' of poverty in the 1960s.

This does not, of course, mean that research based on low incomes has been invalid. It does, however, tend to obscure other issues which the study of 'poverty' has been concerned with. The problems of poor areas are among the problems which researchers lost sight of. The effect of doing research on poverty in terms of individuals has been to change the way that poverty is understood, and often what it was about poverty that excited concern in the first place.

Part Three
Poverty as economic position

SIX

Economic resources

Income, expenditure and wealth

Resources are generally interpreted in terms of income and wealth. Income is what comes in – the flow of resources. Expenditure is what goes out. Wealth is a stock of goods, including both things with a monetary value, like bank accounts and pension rights, and things that can be bought and sold, like housing or clothing.

Most poverty research focuses on income or expenditure rather than wealth. Both income and expenditure are related to the flow of resources. Income is more commonly used in research, because information about income is more commonly available, but the arguments about whether expenditure is preferable to income are specialised, and often subtle. Expenditure is closely related to consumption – how a person obtains goods, services and commodities. Stein Ringen suggests that 'Poverty can be defined and measured either directly (in terms of consumption) or indirectly (in terms of income)'.[63] Because consumption is more closely related to need, he suggests, it is more 'direct' than the use of income. Measuring consumption is arguably a more practical approach for measurement of poverty in developing countries, where the nature of the informal economy means it may be easier to examine aspects of consumption (like nutrition) than formal income. But similar arguments have also been applied in developed countries. A recent report by the Institute for Fiscal Studies has modelled poverty in the UK in terms of expenditure rather than income. They argue that expenditure patterns do not show the same short-term fluctuations that income does, and that using figures for expenditure may be more reliable as a guide to people's resources over time.[64] (Their approach seems to show more long-term poverty than income-based measures do, which makes it unlikely that the UK government is going to welcome it.)

By contrast with income, expenditure and consumption, much less is made of wealth, and on the face of the matter that seems odd. The places people live in, the goods they are able to use, and the clothes they wear are crucial for the way they live. However, there are several problems in focusing on wealth:

- Ownership is not a good guide to the use of resources. People can own things but not be able to use them. People's pension rights matter, but they cannot necessarily be used or realised, and knowing that someone has rights which will be worth something in 20 years' time does not tell us very much about their welfare now. Conversely, people can use things they do not own. A person who rents a house has more or less the same value as someone who owns it, and the difference in wealth is not reflected in the difference in lifestyle. Richard Titmuss argued that resources matter less than 'command over resources'[65] – what people are able to do with them.

- Some things cannot reasonably be traded. People do not trade their wedding rings or jewellery if they can avoid it.
- Market value is not a very good guide to how important something is. The value of furniture has little relationship to its use. Second-hand clothing has a very low value, but lacking clothing is a clear indicator of poverty.

In developed economies, consequently, income tends to be referred to much more than wealth is. On the face of the matter, income does not give a very clear indication of how people will live, but data are widely available and fairly reliable. In developing countries, too, wealth is referred to less often than income. The case for this approach is less clear cut. It is true that wealth is complicated and difficult to measure; even if people in developing countries own land, they do not necessarily have the legal title to it. (This limits their command over resources, because they cannot raise finance on the basis of their property.) But income fluctuates unpredictably, and accumulated resources are an indicator of how things have worked out over a period. It may be possible in those circumstances to take possessions into account more effectively than daily income. Caroline Moser has argued for an approach based on an understanding of poor people's use of assets and housing.[66] The 'asset vulnerability framework' has been influential in the development of recent work to promote sustainable livelihoods.

Income and wealth are not the only types of resources. People draw on the resources of family, friends and communities; most of us are profoundly affected by the position of our families and those closest to us, and, however convenient or agreeable we find the idea that we are individual and independent, it does not really reflect the way that most people live their lives. The idea of 'social capital' has been put to try to capture the impact of some of these resources.[67] Social capital refers to the value of networks of social interaction and support which reside in these social relationships. (There are obvious problems in the concept of social capital: it is not really 'capital', and it cannot be redistributed or expended. It is possible to attach monetary values to many of these activities, because people who do not get them through social relationships have to pay for them, but it does not always make sense to do it. The importance of the idea of social capital has been political: it tells politicians and decision makers that there may be intangible benefits which they are otherwise likely to ignore. In that respect, the idea of social capital has been hugely beneficial in international debates on development.)

For many people, poverty boils down, more or less, to not having enough money. Lack of money means lack of resources; lack of resources tends to imply either a low standard of living, or an inability to meet needs. Paul Ashton writes:

Deprivation is surely about 'essential' needs that are unmet. This may be due to a lack of money resources – but it need not be (since adequate resources may be misspent). Poverty, on the other hand, must refer to a lack of the money necessary to meet those needs.[68]

This can be interpreted in two ways. If Ashton is trying to say that poverty depends on the relationship between needs and resources, that is pretty much equivalent to the way that the idea of 'needs' was interpreted in Chapter Four. Needs are not just problems: they depend on a relationship between problems and responses. It is also possible to read this, however, as a statement that poverty is about the lack of money. This is not a view that everyone shares, but it is certainly common. At times, it seems that the indicators we use for poverty depend on a similar view. The US poverty line is a fairly crude monetary target; the World Bank describes poverty as living on less than a dollar a day, or two dollars a day. When the *International Declaration* states that 'Poverty is primarily an income- or resource-driven concept', it reinforces that perception.

If poverty boils down to a lack of money, the problem is money, not the other aspects of poverty. That means that:

- people can be poor without actually being in need – the test is whether they have enough money to maintain their welfare, not whether they are lacking specific things. If needs are met from other people's resources, such as family relationships or charity, people can still be said to be poor. An example might be a student on a low income;
- people can be poor without being disadvantaged (for example, because other people are just as poor);
- people can be poor without being socially excluded (for example, an older person on a low income who has a network of social support); or
- people can be poor and still be able to participate in society (for example, people in a deprived minority group who rely on each other for social contact and support).

All of these points are arguable. Need, disadvantage, exclusion and the inability to participate might be a consequence of not having enough money, but none of them has to be. If you think poverty means that people do not have enough money, you should not find any of these statements problematic. If you do think there is something wrong with them, it is most likely because you do not think that poverty is just about resources. That does not mean that money is not relevant, but it is not all that matters.

How much is enough?

This book is concerned with the idea of poverty, rather than poverty in one country. It would make very little sense to focus too closely on a single, universal standard of income (like a dollar or two dollars a day). The amount of money that is enough in one place is not going to be the same in other places. For one thing, prices differ. When international organisations like the UNDP or the World Bank compare countries, they generally convert currency not in terms of the exchange rates, but the 'purchasing power parity', trying to gauge how much money is really worth in different countries. The conversion is useful for some purposes, but not for all. There are lots of items, like housing, health and education, where local variations in price make all the difference to the cost for the people who need them.

There are some generalisations we can make.

- *People's needs differ in different countries.* The need for fuel, or clothing, or the quality of building needed to protect people against the elements, is not the same in every place. People in Northern Europe need waterproof shoes; they do not generally need mosquito nets.
- *Social norms are different.* This also means that the commodities that people use are different. What passes for food, housing, fuel or transport depends on the expectations and rules which apply in different countries.
- *Prices vary.* The price of goods depends on the resources available to other people, including people who are not poor. As the demand for goods increases, so does the price. Housing and land prices, in particular, depend heavily on the resources available to other people. This generally means that these resources are less available to poor people in richer countries.
- *The same things do not have to be paid for everywhere.* Goods which are distributed through the market in some countries are not necessarily distributed through the market in others. Many countries now have education provided by the state, without fee. Several, but many fewer, have state-provided medical care (providing a value equivalent to the cost of medical insurance). Other essentials could be provided publicly, though it is rare: a very small number of local administrations offer district heating schemes in place of fuel.

There have been some interesting attempts to apply standards which vary according to social conditions. One is the 'poverty line' in the US. The US poverty line is based mainly on the cost of food; food is assumed to take up a third of the budget of poor people. The justification for this approach rests in the idea of a relationship between food and poverty, originally put by the German economist Engel and developed by Molly Orshansky.[69] It is based on the simple, but generally valid, observation that the poorer people are, the higher the proportion of their income which has to be spent on food. People living on a dollar a day generally spend about 70-80% of their income on food.[70] Of course, the amounts that people spend on food vary, according to culture, diet and personal taste, but the variation is not as large between individuals on similar incomes as it is between richer and poorer people. Expenditure on food can be charted, then, as a proportion of overall income, and when it rises above a certain proportion, it indicates that the person is poor.

The other main approach is the test of income used in the EU. This looks at the income of people on low incomes in relation to the bulk of the population. The median income is the income received by someone in the middle of the income distribution: half the population receives less than the median, half receives more. The European measure does not mean, as some commentators in the press seem to suggest, that making some people rich will make other people poorer. The median income falls, not among rich people, but among lower-paid workers; poor people are not being compared to rich people, but to people on a limited extra income.

The standard that has been most widely used has been 50% of the median income. 50% is an arbitrary figure – the researchers who developed the measure tried levels of 40, 50 and 60% to see what looked most plausible, and 50% was easiest to calculate.[71] In the past few years, 60% of the median has been used more often. This is partly because a large number of people in marginal circumstances were being left out, and partly because researchers wanted a more generous standard, but the decisive issue was probably pressure within the EU from the UK. The British government had made an initial mistake by using 50% of the mean instead of the median (the mean is higher). They wanted to move to using the median instead, but were afraid they would be accused of massaging the figures. (Students can take some comfort from this; government departments make the same sort of mistake in basic mathematics that the rest of us do.) They opted, in consequence, for 60%.

The European standard does mean that poverty is being defined in terms of inequality. By definition, 50% of the population fall above the median, so the greatest number of people who could ever be poor is 50% of the population. There are countries, like Brazil and Mexico, where it has been said quite plausibly that more than half the population is poor. By the test applied in Europe, that is impossible. As the EU gets bigger, taking in more, poorer countries, the indicator may not be sustainable.

Resources and inequality

People tend to be poorer in more unequal countries, and countries which are poorer tend to have greater inequality (see Box 6). However, the relationship of poverty to economic inequality is not straightforward. Discussions of equality and inequality are bedevilled by a common confusion, which assumes that people are unequal because they are different. This is not what 'inequality' means. Men and women are different, and people of different nationalities may be different, but that is not what makes them unequal. People are unequal when one person has an advantage over another. Differences in the amount of money people have generally mean that the person with more money has an advantage, because someone with more money can out-bid someone with less for the same resources. If we want to understand, for example, why people are homeless, it generally follows from the simple fact that there are not enough houses to live in. Housing is distributed in the market, which means that people with more money get houses. People with less money get houses which are less satisfactory, and if there are not enough houses, someone will get left out at the bottom. (There is nothing about this arrangement which is particularly surprising; it is just the way things work. Systems which try to distribute housing beyond the market are subject to the same kinds of process. The core problem, in most countries, is the shortage of housing. The main qualification to that statement is that there are also countries where the shortage is not simply a problem of housing, but the distribution of land.)

Economic inequality is of considerable importance to people's command over resources. There are some issues where prices are set on world markets, which are not much affected by other people in the same locality: but the position of other people affects the kinds of goods which are sold locally, the availability of amenities like health care, education and transport, and the price of many items. I have made the case that prices vary, depending on the circumstances and conditions of other people in society. Food prices tend to depend on national and international markets, reflecting the cost of production and global distribution. But the kinds of foodstuffs which people can buy also depend on local distribution networks, and those networks depend on other people around them; poor people tend to pay more for food, because they cannot buy in bulk, and have to use more accessible but more expensive local stores. Access to quality goods relies on there being a market for such goods, and conversely access to poor-quality food aimed at poor people depends on the local market. 'Poverty goods' are the sort of things that mainly poor people use – things like second-hand items, cheaper fuels or cheap cuts of meat, and services like pawnbrokers, buses or launderettes. American economists refer to the apparent problem of the 'income elasticity of the poverty line'[72]: that the need for minimum income seems to go up when other people's income does. That is exactly what we ought to expect. But there is no fixed standard of income – like the US poverty line, or the World Bank's test of a dollar a day – which takes this into account.

Both command over resources, and the ability to meet needs, are affected by inequality. This is central to the argument that poverty needs to be understood in terms of 'economic distance', which is the rationale for the EU's approach to poverty. O'Higgins and Jenkins write:

> Virtually all definitions of the poverty threshold used in developed economies in the last half-century or so have been concerned with establishing the level of income necessary to allow access to the minimum standards of living considered acceptable in that society at that time. In consequence, there is an inescapable connection between

poverty and inequality: certain degrees or dimensions of inequality ... will lead to people being below the minimum standards acceptable in that society. It is this 'economic distance' aspect of inequality that is poverty. This does not mean that there will always be poverty when there is inequality: only if the inequality implies an economic distance beyond the critical level.[77]

'Economic distance' means that people are unable to afford what other people can afford; either the market does not cater for them, or it caters on terms that they cannot meet. This means that there can never be a fixed, universal standard of resources, applicable to everyone: understanding people's resources always depends on the economic context in which the resources are used.

Box 6: Inequality in different countries

Table 6.1 shows the gap between the poorest and richest people in several countries.[73] Richer countries tend, overall, to be less unequal than poor ones, because the poorest people in very poor countries have very little indeed. There was once a suggestion of a 'U curve'. Poor countries begin as fairly equal; they become unequal in the course of development; and they grow more equal as resources increase.[74] This pattern seems to characterise the transitions between the poorest countries (such as those in Sub-Saharan Africa), middle-income countries like those in South America, and the richest countries in Europe. The relationship is not straightforward, however. Economic development does not spread its benefits evenly. Some countries develop by extending the scope and inclusion of the formal economy, which leads to greater equality, but others largely do it by enriching areas where modern economic production is already well established, and this can exacerbate inequalities.[75] That means that opposite trends are possible; some countries will grow more equal, and others less equal, as development proceeds. Todaro and Smith are sceptical that there is any patterned relationship.[76]

Table 6.1: Inequality in income or consumption

Country	Rank on the Human Development Index	Ratio of richest fifth to the poorest fifth
Sweden	2	4
US	8	8.4
UK	12	7.2
France	16	5.6
Chile	43	18.7
Brazil	72	31.5
Turkey	88	7.7
China	94	10.7
South Africa	119	33.6
Sierra Leone	177	57.6

Economic circumstances, or economic indicators?

Focusing on income points to three main concepts, all of which overlap with other ideas of poverty. One is command over resources. Income is not equivalent to command over resources, but it is the best proxy we have. The second is economic distance, which again income reflects, however imperfectly. The third is the 'standard of living', which was referred to in Chapter Four when considering patterns of deprivation. Standards of living are determined by a relationship between resources and needs. At the same time, the definition used by International Labour Organization describes the standard of living as something 'measured in terms of income or consumption'.[78] That seems to treat income and consumption as being in some way equivalent. Ringen's argument that measures of consumption are more 'direct'[79] only applies if we accept the idea that poverty is about need, not about economic resources. This is not a position that everyone accepts. The most basic flaw in the distinction between 'direct' and 'indirect' measures, though, is that neither income nor consumption sums up everything we need to know about poverty or people's standard of living. These are indicators, not measures. Every statistic is indirect.

There are considerable reservations to make about the idea that poverty can be summed up in terms of a lack of money. The idea is not untenable, but it excludes so many other significant issues that it becomes uninteresting, distracting attention from the things that matter. The same reservations do not apply if we want to use money as an indicator of poverty, rather than a definition of the idea of poverty. Compared to most of the alternatives, income is a very good indicator of poverty. People on low incomes are likely (but not certain) to have other problems. Because income is necessary to meet needs, it is likely that someone on a low income will have unmet needs. It acts, equally, as an indicator of disadvantage, and of the problems in participating in society. At the same time, it is proof of none of these things, because people can have other resources, and other access to social networks. Economic resources have to be kept in perspective.

SEVEN

Class

The idea of 'class' is used in three main ways. The first is the Marxist sense, which understands class in terms of relationship to the means of production. This includes the 'bourgeoisie', who own the means of production, and the 'proletariat', who work for them. Marx thought that, within time, only these two classes would be left. He was wrong about that, as he was about many things[80], but that does not mean that his concept of class is not useful. People form classes depending on their relationship to the labour market: there is a difference between people who are employed, those who are not employed, and those who are 'marginally employed', hovering between both.

The second use of the term is in the Weberian sense. Weber understood class as a description of people with a common economic position. This includes the Marxist idea of class, but it goes much wider: it can be argued that many other groups have a common economic position, such as older people, public housing tenants, or disabled people.

The third use of 'class' is probably the most common: it is the view of class as socioeconomic status. Class is defined by occupation, and treated as a mixture of social standing and the expectation of economic reward associated with the occupation. This chapter is concerned with the economic position of people in poverty, and this understanding of class is not always relevant to those arguments. For anyone who is looking at empirical evidence about class, however, it tends to come in terms of the third definition, rather than the first two.

Poverty and the formal economy

In developing countries, one of the key determinants of whether or not people are poor is whether they can be said to have a relationship to the formal economy. This is reflected in the difference between rural and urban economies – poorer countries tend to be much less urbanised, because their formal economies are underdeveloped – but it extends beyond that. People at the margins of the formal economy, like subsistence farmers, have to grow their food, or barter it. Because their capacity is limited, and because they are not able to trade on adequate terms, their economic position is very weak. When they move from subsistence farming to trade, they can earn money, but they earn most effectively if they specialise in one sort of production or another. When people move into a market economy, they may become more vulnerable, but their income and command over resources generally improves.

We know, from the experience of developed economies, that engagement in the formal economy is not enough. It seems to be true that people who are engaged in the formal economy are better off than those who are excluded, though arguably this is circular – we suppose they are better off because they have more formal income, marked by GDP. Within formal economies, however, there are at least three other classes who are vulnerable to poverty. The first class consists of people on benefits, who are effectively outside the labour market. The receipt of benefits means that they have money, and they are still engaged in the formal economy – their position may not be good, but no one is going to argue that it is as bad as that of people in developing countries who have no system of benefits to draw on. The second class consists of people who are engaged in the labour market, but whose position is insecure. This is not the same as being low paid, but it tends to go together with low pay. Economic insecurity is still better than a low standard of living, but the practical experience of insecurity means, for many, that they will have extended periods on low incomes. The figures in the UK show that more than half the population has been on a low income (below 60% of the median income) for at least one year in the course of the previous thirteen.[81] The position of insecure labour has sometimes been described in terms of a 'dual labour market'. The idea rests on a distinction between the type and character of labour undertaken by people in different parts of the economy, and points to the consistent disadvantages suffered by certain categories of worker.

The third class lies between the other two. At first sight, there hardly seems to be room for there to be any category between people who are insecure and people on benefits, but the conditions are there. The position has been called 'sub-employment'[82]; it refers to people who have a marginal position in the labour market. Marginal groups typically include migrant workers, single parents, some disabled people, and many people with low employment status or skills, who may find themselves employed only casually, intermittently or for limited periods of time. Their work is of low status and earning power; when work is scarce, they are likely to be unemployed. As a result, they are likely to move through various types of ephemeral labour, including temporary employment, casual labour and work in which they are unable to maintain any tenure, as well as experiencing periodic spells of unemployment.

The concept is credible and instantly recognisable, but the evidence on patterns of sub-employment is thin. Because sub-employment is ephemeral, it is difficult to identify. It cannot be classified in terms of a consistent type of employment – the kind of evidence which is used to posit a dual labour market; rather, it has to be understood in dynamic terms, through analysis of employment histories, of the kind undertaken by Morris and Irwin.[83] Some of the evidence on benefit receipt can be used to support the argument: some people move in and out of dependency with varying frequency.[84] Some are repeated short-term claimants, implying a pattern of casual work; some move seasonally; others have a slower, pendulum movement between dependency and low-paid employment, a position which is more consistent with a vulnerable position in a dual labour market. Somewhere between these positions is the irregular, unpredictable pattern over the short- to medium-term pattern consistent with sub-employment.

The economic position of the poor

If poverty is about low income, lack of resources or people's standard of living, then the idea that poor people share a common economic position becomes a tautology. Saying that people have a common economic position does not necessarily mean that they are in the same circumstances; it means that there is something about their circumstances which applies to each of them. This might include some of the factors considered before, like the stability of people's income, regular employment or dependency. But the idea extends to many others. Older people are one example. The idea that disabled people can be thought of as a class comes from Peter Townsend, who made the point after research pointed to low incomes and limited opportunities.[85]

It is not helpful to pretend that there is a single, authoritative description of 'classes' in this sense. What we can do, instead, is to look at some of the key dimensions along which a range of classes might be distinguished. They include:

- *Employment, earnings and the labour market* – the issues considered in the previous section. A typical distinction lies between people in secure employment, insecure employment, sub-employment and non-employment.
- *The distribution of resources.* This is commonly represented as a distinction between 'rich' and 'poor' people, but there is a wide spectrum of positions in between: information about the distribution of income commonly divides the population into 'quintiles', or fifths. (In the UK, the lowest two fifths of households are mainly people on benefits.)
- *Housing classes.* Rex and Moore, in a well-known study, suggested that it was possible to distinguish the economic position of people with different housing tenures[86], a position partly justified by their differential wealth and security, but also by the differences in standards of living. The main distinction falls between home owners and those who rent, but there are subdivisions in each category, including for example those who own their home with or without mortgages or loan finance, and those who rent from public and private landlords. There are also marginal tenures, and people excluded from the main categories include people who live in non-standard buildings (such as caravans, trailers and boats), squatters and homeless people.
- *The receipt of benefits.* The distinction between benefit recipients and others will be returned to in Chapter Nine, in the discussion of 'dependency'. It is also possible to make distinctions between older people, long-term benefit recipients (like disabled people) and short-term benefit recipients (like unemployed people).

- *Distinctions between communities and geographic areas.* People in certain geographic areas can find themselves in a different economic position. At a general level, it is possible to make distinctions between urban and rural environments, and between people in richer and poorer neighbourhoods.
- *Gender.* There is an argument for saying that poverty is 'feminised'.[87] Women are more likely to find themselves in economic and domestic circumstances which lead to poverty, and most poor people are women. However, it does not follow that women are poor; in developed economies, most are not.
- *Minority ethnic groups.* This is one of the most contentious classifications. Debates in the US[88] (and increasingly in the UK[89]) are often conducted under the assumption that poverty mainly affects people from racial minorities. In the US, this is usually applied to African Americans and people of Hispanic origin, but neither group is predominantly poor or dependent on welfare. In the UK, similar assumptions are made about people described as 'Black'.[90] (If 'Black' means people of West Indian or African descent, it is inaccurate; those groups are disadvantaged, but they are mainly not poor.[91] If 'Black' is intended to cover a broader range of minority groups from Africa and Asia, the term fails to distinguish people in significantly different circumstances.) The strongest case in the UK relates to people of Pakistani and Bangladeshi descent, because the majority of people in those two groups are on a low income.[92] It is possible to extend the argument to gypsy travellers.[93] There are reasons, however, to be cautious. As a general proposition, it is often true that some minorities are more vulnerable to poverty than the rest of the population. That is not the same as saying that they are poor; most are not. Minority communities are very diverse, and that diversity is reflected in a wide dispersion of economic circumstances and opportunities. The effect of assuming disadvantage is often to reinforce negative stereotypes and stigma.

There is a wide range of potential classifications, and there is not much to be said that applies to them all. All of these approaches suffer from the problem that the categorisations are likely to be inconsistent with the circumstances of some individuals. In any broadly classified group – disabled people, tenants, minority ethnic groups – there will be richer and poorer people, people who are relatively advantaged and people who are disadvantaged. Further, the way in which the groups are classified inevitably glosses over other issues. Economic position is primarily determined for households rather than individuals. Feminist critics have argued that this tends to conceal the position of people *within* the household, and in particular the disadvantaged position of women.[94]

Because there are so many alternative classifications, it is not possible to point to any one of them and say that it represents the economic position of the poor. In any classification of this sort, 'poverty' refers to people at the bottom, and it remains true that 'poverty' is a normative concept. Advocates of particular approaches – for example, those who focus on minority groups, or those who focus on geographic disadvantage – are usually trying to make a moral case for attention to the people who are disadvantaged.

Opportunities and life chances

The model of the 'web of deprivation', introduced in Chapter Four, suggests that poverty is a shifting, fluctuating set of conditions. The idea of 'class' depends on the opposite view. Class is generally taken to be a long-term, underlying category which reflects patterns of life, opportunities and life chances. This is conventionally represented in terms of socioeconomic status. Including issues like occupation, education and social standing are ways of trying to capture the disposing factors which lie under the surface.

This approach sounds initially implausible, and it has been subject to a wide range of criticisms. In political debates, the idea that life chances are patterned and determined often seems at odds with arguments for individualism, opportunity and social mobility. In academic circles, 'postmodern' approaches have argued for a less preconceived, more fluid approach to social analysis, while critical groups, including feminists and anti-racists, have argued that an emphasis on traditional forms of class tends to disguise the importance of other social divisions. The core argument for keeping the idea of 'class' is that it points to things that other approaches fail to spot.

The principle is clearly demonstrated by the relationship between health and social class.[95] There is a relationship between income and wealth on one hand and health on the other (see Box 7). But health issues are not just about people's present experience; they also reflect previous experience. The problems of malnutrition presented in Box 4 – underweight, wasting and stunting – are an example. There are problems like this in developed economies, but it is difficult to show the relationship clearly, because so many people pass through poverty for limited periods of time.

There are clear differences in the incidence of ill health by social class (see Box 7). People in lower social classes, including children, are more likely to suffer from infective and parasitic diseases, pneumonia, poisonings or violence. Adults in lower social classes are more likely, in addition, to suffer from cancer, heart disease and respiratory disease. The pattern is not the same for every disease: for example, while schizophrenia is most common in the lowest social class, depression is much more common in social class II. Health depends on a wide range of factors, including lifestyle, nutrition, education and behaviour over time. Social class is a useful indicator of those kinds of issue, while economic position is not.

There is a connection between poverty and ill health, but the connection is not always clear. Much depends on what we understand poverty to be. If it is a set of problems, like a low standard of living, low income or deprivation, poverty is potentially ephemeral. If poverty is about social relationships, like dependency

Box 7: Inequality and health

The literature identifying ill health with social class in developed countries is well established. A long series of research reports has charted patterns of inequality in relation to social class.[96] Table 7.1 shows, as an example, the long-term trends in coronary heart disease in the UK.[97]

Table 7.1: Coronary heart disease, per 1,000,000 people, by social class and gender, UK

Social class	Women aged 35-64			Men aged 35-64		
	1976-81	1981-85	1986-92	1976-81	1981-85	1986-92
I/II	39	45	29	246	185	160
III non-manual	56	57	39	382	267	162
III manual	85	67	59	309	269	231
IV/V	105	76	78	363	293	266
Ratio of IV/V: I/II	2.69	1.69	2.69	1.48	1.58	1.66

It is difficult to classify socioeconomic status in developing countries in the same terms, and much of the literature focuses instead on the relationship between resources and health. Researchers for the World Bank have suggested using assets, instead of income, as a proxy measure; the assets they refer to include electricity, possession of a car and connection to a sewer.[98] Figures for wealth are intended as a proxy for patterns of long-term deprivation. Table 7.2 shows the relationship between the distribution of wealth and infant mortality in six countries.[99] People are ranked by deciles, according to their accumulated possessions rather than their income. Each decile represents one tenth of the population, staged from the poorest to the richest. Children in the poorest tenth of the population are three times more likely to die in Bangladesh, and seven times more likely to die in Uganda.

Table 7.2 Percentage of children born in the previous five years and no longer living, by wealth (1999)

Decile	1	2	3	4	5	6	7	8	9	10
Bangladesh	19	13	10	9	8	10	7	9	9	6
Indonesia	25	14	8	6	6	5	5	5	4	4
Madagascar	25	14	13	10	10	10	10	9	8	8
Pakistan	18	10	10	9	9	7	8	7	7	6
Tanzania	49	18	13	14	11	10	8	7	7	9
Uganda	48	19	16	14	13	9	12	9	9	7

and exclusion, there is a link to poor health, but some of the issues are circular –
like the link between disability and poor health – and others are also short term.
Poverty is most clearly linked to ill health when it implies prolonged and serious
deprivation. However, poverty takes different forms, and the link is not
straightforward. Shifting the debate to 'class' is intended to identify the issues
which matter over time.

The underclass

Many understandings of poverty treat poverty as a negative concept, a position
occupied by people because of what they do not have. But there is another view
of the poor, which suggests that they are poor because of the position they do
occupy, not because of the space they don't. On the face of the matter, poverty
and class are closely linked. This relationship has been expressed in several ways,
most directly in terms of an 'underclass'. The 'underclass' is composed of people
whose economic position is not simply poor, but effectively excluded from the
mainstream of economic production.[100] The underclass is a class, in the formal
sense, because exclusion defines a set of economic and social relationships. A
Marxist class analysis defines people's class in terms of their relationship to the
means of production; there must then be some distinction between the 'working
class' and those who have no direct relationship to the industrial system. A
Weberian approach makes the same kind of distinction, though it might also
suggest a number of underclasses. The classification of occupations by
socioeconomic status starts from the premise that status groups are primarily
defined in terms of occupational categories, and it follows that those with no
occupational category are likely to fall below the levels occupied by those who
have. The 'underclass' is a socioeconomic grouping falling beneath the criteria
by which other socioeconomic groups are classified.

On the face of the matter, this looks straightforwardly like a question for social
science. But the idea of the underclass has been abused by right-wing critics
prepared to condemn the poor for their poverty. The kind of attack which was
commonplace in the 1960s has resurfaced in full flow. Auletta, for example,
associates the underclass with 'violence, arson, hostility and welfare
dependency'.[101] Lister records comparisons with disease ('plague' and 'cancer')
as well as various references to animals.[102] The element of moral judgement has
tainted the debate, and it makes it difficult to discuss the issue without being
vulnerable to the accusation of blaming the victims. The idea of the underclass
is associated by some commentators on the left with some of the anti-welfare
literature from the US.[103] A common line of attack has been that the category
is meaningless:

> 'Underclass' is a destructive and misleading label that lumps together
> different people who have different problems ... the latest of a series

of popular labels ... that focuses on individual characteristics and thereby stigmatises the poor for their poverty.[104]

Several commentators take the view that the idea is offensive. Gans writes:

the term has taken on so many connotations of undeservingness and blameworthiness that it has become hopelessly polluted in meaning, ideological overtone and implications, and should be dropped.[105]

If the issue is just that people think the term is insulting, however, we have the same problem with many other ways of talking about poverty. David Matza argues that people at the bottom of the social structure are generally stigmatised, and any term which is used becomes over time a term of abuse.[106] The problem with poor people is not the label; it is that they are at the bottom. Lister argues, more subtly, that 'Othering' the poor – treating the poor as something different from the rest of us – is basic to their stigmatisation.[107] Arguments which seem to be about a dispassionate assessment of persistent poverty may be taken to show that poor people are inferior beings.

There is a serious side, though, to the idea of the underclass. The idea was initially intended to point our attention to an area which was all too frequently left out of conventional class analysis; the term was first used by social scientists on the political left.[108] It made it possible to start comparing the position of poor people over time with other groups of people in society. These issues need to be thought about without the political claptrap that usually goes along with the term.

Attempts to explain poverty in terms of an underclass rely on the idea that people can be said to be poor over a long period of time. This was the subject of an influential paper in the US by Bane and Ellwood. They argued:

Most of the people helped by programs to aid the economically disadvantaged use them only briefly. But the bulk of resources almost certainly go to a much smaller group of people who have very long stays in poverty.[109]

This is half right. Snapshots do not necessarily reflect the 'spell' or period of time during which people are dependent, some people remain in poverty for much longer than others, and the picture of poverty taken for any particular moment tends to be distorted by the disparity between different people's experiences. However, there are two qualifications to make about Bane and Ellwood's argument. The first is that when they say that some people in the US are poor for 'very long' periods, they are talking about 10 years or more. This is a very long time, but they are not talking about people being poor all their lives, and they are certainly not showing that it passes from one generation to another. The second is that they could not, within the framework they used, reflect the importance of the economic background over time. In a depressed economy, people are poor and dependent for longer periods. When economies recover, changing employment opportunities lead to marked differences in dependency rates.

The main reservation to make about the attempt to analyse poverty in terms of an underclass is that it does not describe the experience of poverty very accurately. Poverty is a complicated, shifting set of circumstances. Class is generally seen as a consistent pattern of relationships underlying a constellation of outcomes and life chances over time. The general experience of developed countries has been that relatively few people, with the main exception of older people, stay poor for very long periods. Beyond that, among people who are poor, there is also a considerable amount of movement and change.[110] That is not necessarily inconsistent with class theory: issues like sub-employment and marginal labour also imply frequent changes in people's circumstances. It does, however, raise questions about the idea of the underclass as a group of people with shared values, behaviour or characteristics. If the idea of the underclass means anything, it is an economic position, not a static category.

Part Four
Poverty and social relationships

EIGHT

Social exclusion

The idea of exclusion

Many authors have written about social exclusion in recent years. Most have been less concerned to understand the concept than they have to impose their own meanings on it. Although the idea seemed new to many people in the 1990s, it has grown out of an ancient tradition in Continental Europe.

The idea developed mainly in the context of French social policy. Social policy in English-speaking countries has tended to focus on the position of the poor. By contrast, French social policy has never mainly been concerned with 'poverty', and until fairly recently, it was relatively rare to see books that were much concerned with the idea. The central concept of French social policy is not the 'welfare state' – when the term is used, it tends to be seen as negative, a bit like the English phrase 'nanny state' – but the concept of 'solidarity'. The idea is commonly attributed by sociologists to Durkheim[111], but that is misleading: the idea dates back to at least the 16th century, it features in the Napoleonic Code, and it became firmly established as part of political discussion in the 1840s. It also came, significantly, to be a central part of Catholic social teaching. That teaching begins from the proposition that people live in families and communities; they are linked by a network of relationships and obligations.[112] Solidarity refers to the responsibility that people have for each other. The *Code de Sécurité Sociale* takes this principle as the starting point for social security provision. Solidarity is mainly taken to refer to mutual aid through insurance.[113]

The main thrust of French social policy after World War II was to extend the coverage of social insurance to everyone, through a process of *généralisation*[114] – the gradual, progressive inclusion of people in networks of solidarity. The process was complete by 1974; everyone who could be included in an insurance programme was. Unfortunately, people can only be included in insurance if they are able to pay contributions. This was the situation in which René Lenoir wrote *Les exclus*, arguing that one French person in ten had been 'excluded', in the sense of being left out.[115] The excluded were those who did not have the protection that others had – the people who were not included in relationships of solidarity. If solidarity is defined in terms of the responsibilities which people experience within certain types of social groupings, some people must be considered to fall outside the scope of those responsibilities. At the extremes, people who are excluded will have very few social relationships – the archetypal 'excluded' person is the *clochard* or tramp – but there are degrees of exclusion, because people can be part of some groups and not others. Exclusion means, rather, that people are not part of a pattern of relationships in which they feel obligated to others, and others feel obligated towards them.

The idea of 'social exclusion' gained currency in the European Union as a different way of discussing the issues of poverty. It happened partly because of the influence of the idea in France, and partly because the British government of the time had made a determined attempt to prevent discussion of 'poverty' in European settings. The Tiemann report took a pragmatic view: if 'poverty' was not an acceptable term, they could always use 'exclusion' instead.[116] That is why various recent treaties in the EU refer to exclusion but not to poverty.

The meaning of exclusion

The first, core meaning of the idea was that some people were left out: that they were not part of the solidaristic social networks that applied to others. The idea was hugely influential in France, and after a short time it was starting to be used in a variety of ways. Exclusion might be taken in a negative sense, contrasting those who are within the bounds of social networks unfavourably with those who are outside them. It can carry the imputation of deviance. People who are excluded from society are sometimes described as *inadaptés*, which might be taken to be not just those who are left out, but also those who are maladjusted.[117] A French government circular in 1976 referred to exclusion as another way of understanding what in Britain might have been called the 'problem family':

> families generally described as 'problem families' or 'anti-social', or more objectively, families which are 'marginal', 'excluded' or in the 'fourth world', who appear temporarily unable to resolve the problems they are confronted with.[118]

This points to a second understanding of the idea of exclusion. At first it meant people who were not protected. This became extended to people who were not part of society – in other words, people who were deviant. In France, this is linked with the idea of 'marginality': 'Deviants and marginals are not forgiven for their refusal to share in the "values of the system"'.[119] In Britain, the idea of exclusion has been compounded with ideas relating to the 'underclass': Tony Blair describes 'exclusion' as:

> a short hand label for what can happen when individuals or areas suffer from a combination of linked problems such as unemployment, poor skills, low incomes, poor housing, high crime environments, bad health and family breakdowns.[120]

The third meaning of exclusion, which follows from this, has been to refer to people who are socially rejected. In France, the term has been applied, for example, to people who are unemployed[121], young offenders[122], or people with

AIDS[123]. We are still talking about people who are not part of society, but they are not left out, or standing outside. They are pushed out.

When the EU took up the idea of exclusion, then, there were already a variety of competing understandings of what the term might mean. It covered people who were left out, people who refused to take part in society, and people who were rejected. The idea of 'exclusion' is very wide.

> Social exclusion affects individuals, groups of people and geographical areas. Social exclusion can be seen, not just in levels of income, but also matters such as health, education, access to services, housing and debt. Phenomena which result from social exclusion therefore include:
> – the resurgence of homelessness
> – urban crises
> – ethnic tension
> – rising long term unemployment
> – persistent high levels of poverty.[124]

The kinds of issue mentioned, like racial issues or urban crises, point generally to the structure of social relationships as the focus for concern.

Academics have tried to reinterpret the idea of exclusion in terms of the sociological literature. Silver, for example, refers to a Marxist concept of exclusion, related to the economy; a Durkheimian model, related to solidarity; and a Weberian model, related to 'specialisation' or the distinct economic and social position of excluded people.[125] As the idea has spread across Europe, it has been forced into the mould of national politics, and now there are almost as many varieties of 'exclusion' as there are of poverty.

Exclusion is different mainly in the prescriptions it offers for policy. If the main issue is that people are excluded from society, they have to be included. When provision was made for social assistance in France in the 1980s, it took a different form from the kind of welfare benefits offered in other countries. The *revenu minimum d'insertion* (RMI) offered a minimum income, but it also made provision for 'insertion', or social inclusion. The RMI was introduced as:

> one of the elements of a general provision in the struggle against poverty, directed toward the suppression of every kind of exclusion, in particular in the fields of education, employment, training, health and housing.[126]

Inclusion had two parts. On one hand, excluded people were expected, as a condition of receiving benefits, to make a contract with society – a 'contract of insertion'. On the other, society, for its part, had to make provision available which was going to lead to social inclusion. The local agency with responsibility for this, the *commission locale d'insertion*, had then to make two sorts of contract. One was the contract with claimants, negotiated with social workers; the other was a series of contracts with agencies, local industries and facilities to provide facilities that people would be able to use, facilities like jobs, training courses, educational opportunities and provision for social support. This approach has been profoundly influential. Schemes modelled on the French RMI have been introduced in Portugal[127], northern Spain[128] and in Italy[129].

'Exclusion' or 'poverty'?

The primary use of the idea of exclusion relates to poverty, because much of the concern with 'solidarity' relates to the availability of systems of support to meet needs. Poverty is not seen simply as a matter of lacking resources; it implies that people who are poor are not protected by solidarity, and so are not fully part of society. The kind of concept of poverty favoured by Townsend is very similar to the idea of social exclusion:

> Individuals, families and groups in the population can be said to be in poverty when they lack the resources to obtain the types of diet, participate in the activities and have the living conditions and amenities which are customary ... in the societies to which they belong.[130]

Townsend's stress on non-participation is directly compatible with the idea of 'exclusion' – indeed, Townsend actually used the idea of exclusion in his classic work on poverty, though without assigning any special importance to it. The mechanisms through which people participate in society develop in terms of the pattern of social networks to which they belong. People who are unable to participate are seen as being on the margins of society, or excluded from it. But the same principles apply to many people who are not 'poor'. The idea of exclusion is used to refer to people in a wide range of conditions related to disadvantage, deprivation or socially undesirable circumstances.

Some people think that exclusion is very different from poverty.[131] The basis for this is a view of poverty as a concept linked with inadequate resources, while exclusion is seen as a relational issue, concerned principally with a person's position in society. But poverty, like exclusion, can be seen in relational terms. The Council of the European Communities has adopted the following definition of poverty:

> The poor shall be taken to mean persons, families and groups of persons where resources (material, cultural and social) are so limited as to exclude them from the minimum acceptable way of life in the member states in which they live.[132]

The idea of exclusion can be difficult to distinguish from that of poverty in this sense.

When we talk about social exclusion we are acknowledging that the problem is no longer simply one of inequity between the top and bottom of the social scale (up/down) but also one of the distance within society between those who are active members and those who are forced towards the fringes (in/out). We are also highlighting the effects of the way society is developing and the concomitant risk of social disintegration and, finally, we are affirming that, for both the persons concerned and the society itself, this is a process of change and not a set of fixed and static situations.[133]

These points are important, but they have all been made about poverty. The first point – that people are marginalised in society – is reflected in the widespread concerns in the literature on poverty with issues like disability (see Box 8) and 'race'. The concern with social disintegration and cohesion is a long-standing concern in discussions about the relationship of poverty to inequality as well as fulminations about the underclass. The dynamic, frequently changing nature of poverty has not been researched as much as the topic merits, but it was strongly emphasised in work on continuities of deprivation[134], and work on studies over time has taken the issue further.[135]

Similarly, the implications of the idea of exclusion for policy do not seem at first sight to be remarkably different from those of poverty. In relation to exclusion, the European Commission has identified three main approaches.[136] The first is that because the problem of exclusion is multi-dimensional, so are the solutions. The pervasive nature of exclusion means that 'preventing and combatting social exclusion calls for an overall mobilisation of efforts and combination of both economic and social measures'.[137] Second, the problems have to be tackled by a partnership between a range of social actors and agencies; this helps to define a role for the non-governmental organisations which have been such a major part of the EUs approach to social policy. Third, people have to be able to participate in the decision-making process, because participation is a central aim in itself of policies against exclusion.[138] There is nothing here which might not be argued in relation to poverty in its broader sense – and indeed, the Commission has itself formerly applied precisely the same approaches in relation to poverty.[139]

Box 8: Disability

The problems of disability relate, not just to physical limitations, but to the effect that they have on the roles of disabled people, people's reactions and on the ability to participate in society. The World Health Organization (WHO) bases its current classification on three main categories:

- problems in bodily function or structure;
- problems relating to activities and
- problems related to social participation.[140]

The WHO has been condemned for not taking the social elements of disability into account.[141] This is unfair: the term 'handicap', which they used for over 30 years, was clearly intended to refer to the same issues as the social model of disability.

International statistics about the prevalence of disability are not available yet, but in their absence Table 8.1 shows some of the WHO estimates.[142]

Table 8.1: WHO estimates of the prevalence of some disabling conditions, 2002 (000s)

Asthma	227,693
Diabetes	181,699
HIV/AIDS	39,395
Epilepsy	38,574
Schizophrenia	25,262
Rheumatoid arthritis	22,732
Alzheimers and other dementias	22,541
Spinal cord injuries	19,359
Intracranial injury	18,715
Parkinson's disease	5,004
Multiple sclerosis	2,380

It is still possible to make three general statements about disability. First, *disability is diverse*. The stereotyped image of a disabled person is probably of someone in a wheelchair, but that is relatively unusual. Disability results from a wide range of circumstances, including conditions like blindness, motor disorders, deafness, inability to sustain a physical effort, epilepsy, mental illness and learning disability. There is a wide range of long-term, limiting diseases, including disorders of the nervous system (like multiple sclerosis and stroke), neuromuscular disorders (like muscular dystrophy and polio), and disorders affecting blood, bones and metabolism.

Second, *most disabled people are old*. This is very clear from national surveys in developed countries. It is not obvious that the same is true of developing countries, because children are much more vulnerable to malnutrition, and parasitic and infective diseases. Global figures for blindness, however, show the same pattern in developing countries: the estimates are that 1.4 million people under the age of 15, 5.2 million people aged between 15 and 49, and 30.3 million over the age of 50 are blind.[143] It is plausible, at least, to suggest that the greater prevalence of disability in elderly people applies across the world.

Third, *disabled people do not have to be poor*. The problems of poverty come about because disabled people are often excluded, economically and socially. Most people become disabled later in life, after a period when they have worked; where there are systems of social protection, it should be possible in principle for provision to be made. In practice, however, though many disabled people are often likely to be left out of the formal economy, poorer people are more vulnerable to disability, and more likely ultimately to find themselves without protection when they become disabled.

Relationships of exclusion

The idea of exclusion has largely supplanted a term that used to be used extensively in the discussion of poverty: the idea of stigma. Poverty has long been seen as a problem which is degrading, humiliating and likely to lead to rejection. In the nineteenth century, the 'stigma of pauperism' was one of the driving forces of policy, used deliberately by the authorities to discourage people from claiming poor relief in the belief that it would strengthen the position of the 'independent labourer'. Independent labourers were also thought of as the 'honest poor'; the idea of stigma was more clearly attached to dependent poverty than to poverty alone, though all poverty might be thought to be stigmatising. The problems of dependent poverty will be considered in Chapter Nine. At this stage, the main issues concern stigma and social rejection.

Stigma has many meanings. A popular sociology book by Goffman slides from one definition to another: he refers to stigma partly as a personal flaw, partly in terms of the feelings of the stigmatised person, and partly as the attitudes of other people towards the stigmatised person.[144] Stigmas attach to many of the circumstances in which people might be poor, as well as to poverty itself; people can be socially rejected for physical differences and mental differences, as well as for moral judgements about their behaviour. In different ways, people who are physically disabled, mentally ill, people with learning disabilities and single parents all suffer from a level of stigmatisation.

People who are poor can be stigmatised for any of these reasons; beyond that, they can be stigmatised for poverty itself. There are strong links between social status, esteem and financial resources. People at the bottom of the heap, however that is defined, are likely to be despised for it. In some societies, people are born into a low status: the position of people in caste societies, like 'untouchables' or fellahin, leads to social exclusion and rejection. In western societies, people are not born into their status, and poverty is often seen as a moral failing. One of many depressing observations about poverty is that poor people are often reluctant to describe themselves as poor, or to acknowledge the term.

There are many different kinds of stigma, and it does not follow that a person who is rejected for one reason should be rejected for others. Unfortunately, we have stepped into a discussion where 'what makes sense' and 'what actually happens' are not always on speaking terms. Debates about poverty are affected by a deep-rooted set of beliefs and attitudes. For centuries, and in many societies besides the industrialised societies of the West, poverty has been associated with immorality, danger, and dirt.[145] The associations are not a product of social conditions in industrial Europe or even the developing world; they stretch back into tribal society and the earliest histories.[146] The link with immorality appears in accusations of dishonesty and sexual misbehaviour. The link with danger appears variously in concerns with crime, infection and a sense of personal threat. The association of poverty with dirt is just as irrational. Orwell wrote:

> It may not greatly matter if the average middle class person is brought
> up to believe that the working classes are ignorant, lazy, boorish and
> dishonest; it is when he is brought up to believe that he is dirty that
> the harm is done.[147]

One of the basic premises of a caste system is that people who work with dirt
have the capacity to pollute people who are clean. Of course, some people work
with dirt, and they get dirty in the process. But the problems of hygiene when
facilities are lacking could also mean that poorer people are more aware of dirt,
not less aware, and that they place a higher value on cleanliness.[148] The persistent
association of poor people with dirt – and the leap to assume that dirty people
should be treated like dirt – is one of the clearest indications that we have left the
world of reason behind.

Some people have taken the view that the construction of social borders and
the process of exclusion is so firmly based that it is close to 'human nature'. That
is difficult to prove or disprove, though even if we accept that the statement is
true, there are two basic objections to that position. The first is that even if
borders occur generally, they do not occur in the same places. Some societies
have divisions based on wealth, some on birth, some on ethnicity. There will be
examples elsewhere where the same obstacles have been overcome, and that
means there must be ways of making society more inclusive. Second, just because
people are that way doesn't mean that it's right. People do reject others, they
rely on stereotypes, they can be self-centred and insensitive. Morality is about
getting people to behave better, and claiming that 'it's human nature' is not a
defence.

We need to recognise that there is a potential contradiction in arguing for
social inclusion and arguing against social borders. The very idea of 'inclusion'
suggests that there are limits – that some people will be included, and others will
not. It is not clear, however, that exclusion from provision – such as the exclusion
of foreigners – has to be accompanied by the kind of stigma and negative
stereotyping considered here. Every government has to consider where the
boundaries will fall – for example, whether people within a state will be included,
whether inclusion extends to outsiders, such as foreigners, and whether
responsibility goes beyond the bounds of the state. The stigmatisation of foreigners
and immigrant minorities is sometimes part of the process, but there is no intrinsic
contradiction in accepting some boundaries while considering stigmatisation to
be unacceptable.

NINE

Dependency

When the issue of poverty is discussed in the popular press, it tends not simply to refer to deprivation or economic resources. More typically, 'the poor' are treated as a class of people who live on welfare benefits. The sociologist Georg Simmel argued that 'poverty', in sociological terms, referred not to all people on low incomes, but to those who were dependent.

> The poor person, sociologically speaking, is the individual who receives assistance because of the lack of means.[149]

Engbersen has described poverty as

> the structural exclusion of citizens from all social participation, along with a situation of dependence in relation to the State.[150]

This is a long-standing association. The link reflects the influence of the English Poor Laws which lasted for 350 years. Poor people were strongly identified with the provision made for them. The influence of the Poor Law was felt in many countries – not only those which had it, like Ireland, but in those which did not, like the US and Australia. Dependency is a major element in the discussion of poverty in the media and popular culture, particularly in discussions from the US.[151] In this discourse, 'the poor ... are increasingly with us, breeding future generations of uneducated bastards dependent on welfare, mugging and drug dealing'.[152]

The link between poverty and dependency relies on some key assumptions about how benefits systems work, and what happens to poor people when they receive them. On one hand, benefit systems are believed to support poor people; on the other, poor people are not able to manage without the benefits. Neither of those propositions is unreasonable, but they are not as circular as they may seem. Benefit systems do support poor people, but they do not only support poor people. Some benefits support poor people along with others, like benefits for older people and children. Some benefits do not support poor people at all: pensions were once the preserve of the privileged, and there are still many benefit systems across the world which depend on contributions and work record. In developing countries, inclusion in social security schemes is still often confined to people in the protected areas of the formal economy, like the civil service or manufacturing industry. The kind of benefits system which is being assumed here is a 'safety net' for people on low incomes. There are now safety nets in most Organisation for Economic Co-operation and Development (OECD) countries, but usually they are only a limited part of the benefit system, for people who do not qualify for other forms of social protection.

The second assumption is that poor people are 'dependent' on the money. Dependency is, in its nature, a relationship: there is someone who is dependent, and another person who is depended on. To say that people are dependent is to say that they receive support from others, and that without that support they would not be able to function. This could mean that all their income comes from benefit, but that is not necessarily true; if there is some kind of minimum income threshold, and people fall below that, their 'dependency' can be for any amount used to top people up to the minimum, because they remain in need until the minimum is met. Most roads are publicly funded, but we do not say that people who drive on them are dependent. Farmers who receive agricultural subsidies, builders who work on construction projects for government, or students who receive bursaries, are not thought of as 'dependent': but unemployed people on government training programmes, welfare recipients who have work or training as a condition of receiving benefits, or people who have to leave their job and claim benefit to look after elderly relatives are. We need to understand that 'dependency' is a contentious, judgemental, highly coloured and prejudicial concept. The term, Fraser and Gordon write, 'leaks a profusion of stigmatizing connotations – racial, sexual, misogynist and more'. [153]

The problem with the idea of 'dependency' is that it carries many more implications than the simple issue of whether money is being transferred. There are three main forms of dependency: financial, physical and psychological. Financial dependency happens where people receive essential financial support. People are physically dependent when the kind of help they receive is to meet their physical needs – for example, washing, dressing, preparing meals. Young children are generally physically dependent; some older people become dependent through disability or mental decline. Psychological dependency is the most contentious category. This can mean that people have psychological needs which have to be met; it can also mean that people in a dependent relationship learn to be dependent, and lose a sense of personal responsibility. These kinds of arguments are commonly made about poor individuals, but the same kinds of arguments about poor countries can be found:

> Huge bureaucracies are financed (with the aid money), corruption and complacency are promoted, Africans are taught to be beggars and not to be independent. ... Africa is like a child that immediately cries for its babysitter when something goes wrong. Africa should stand on its own two feet.[154]

Criticisms of the 'dependency culture' are not really about financial issues. They are much more likely to be criticisms of the attitude and behaviour of people who are poor. The idea that poor people are trapped in a 'dependency culture' has three main components. The first is that they are dependent; second, that they are trapped in their dependency; and third, that they have learned dependent behaviour as a result. We find this sort of statement in several places – one of the best known is Charles Murray's book *Losing ground*[155], and Lawrence Mead's *Beyond entitlement*[156] covers similar ground in different ways – but the arguments have been around for centuries. The phenomenon of modern unemployment was first recorded in Britain after the Napoleonic wars, apparently a problem of the Industrial Revolution, but for some 50 years before that there were complaints about the sort of dependency which has become familiar since. The British Library has a splendid collection of tracts about the Poor Law, which used to belong to Edwin Chadwick, one of the founders of the 1834 reform. From these we can see that a belief that the poor had been corrupted by the Poor Laws began to be expressed in the mid–18th century, and grew from that time onwards. Alcock wrote that

> When the Statute of Elizabeth relieving the Poor first took place, the Burthen was light and inconsiderable. Few applied for relief. It was a Shame and a Scandal for a person to throw himself on a parish ... but the Sweets of Parish-Pay being once felt, more and more Persons soon put in for a share of it. One cried, he as much wanted, and might as well accept it, as another; the Shame grew less and less, and Numbers encouraged and countenanced one another.[157]

Gascoigne, in 1818, stated that only 30 years beforehand,

> A general feeling of self-dependence pervaded the labouring class; that parish relief was considered as disgraceful and disgusting; and that to apply for it, even in old age, was to admit either idleness, improvidence, or extreme misfortune.[158]

Earl Grey believed, in 1834, that

> It was aforetime a shame such as no man could bear, to be dependent upon parochial aid – the name of 'pauper' coming next, in the estimation of the peasant, to that of 'felon'.[159]

We cannot say that people are wrong about dependency just because people have been saying it for a long time, but we can scotch two misconceptions. One is that the problem of dependency – or at least, the assumption that dependency is a problem – is a new phenomenon, in some sense a product of the generous welfare state. Clearly, it is not, because it predates the welfare state by 200 years. The second is that a generation ago, people were ashamed to claim benefits, and that now only old people are ashamed. People have been saying this for centuries, and they cannot all be right. We know from the sequence of these comments that if Alcock was right, Gascoigne was wrong to think it was a new problem in 1818, and if Gascoigne was right in 1818, Earl Grey was wrong in 1834. This seems to be a recurring myth.

Stigma and dependency

Dependency is a highly stigmatised condition. By contrast with the preconception that people are eager to claim and depend on benefits, there is a long-standing problem of people failing to claim the benefits they are entitled to.[160] Part of this has to do with people's lack of knowledge about benefits, and the complexity of the benefits system. There has also been, however, a concern that people fail to claim because of the stigma of claiming – because claiming benefits is seen as degrading, humiliating or shameful.

The issue of stigma overlaps with lots of other issues.[161] Every form of poverty is stigmatised. Some of the conditions which lead to poverty, like unemployment, mental illness and low educational development, are stigmatised. Some of the consequences of poverty, like living in bad housing or being badly fed, are stigmatised. And poverty itself is a stigmatising condition. Poor people are often reluctant to describe themselves as 'poor', because the suggestion is seen in some way as unpleasant, degrading or insulting.

The idea that dependency is stigmatising is not, then, especially surprising: people who are dependent are likely, in the same way, to be in undesirable circumstances and to be socially rejected. Sociologists have argued, though, that dependency is especially stigmatised, because of the relationships which dependency applies. Social relationships rely centrally on exchange, or 'reciprocity'.[162] People need to make a return for the things they receive. In some cases, the return that they make happens over time: children will contribute in the future, older people are usually treated as if they have contributed in the past. In some cases, the returns people make are passed on to others: parents help their children in return for the help that their parents gave them. This is part of the pattern of 'solidarity' referred to in Chapter Eight. But people who fail to make a return are failing to meet their social obligations. Unemployed people are widely rejected because they are seen as a drain on others – a 'public burden'. People who are sick or disabled have allowances made for them in the short term, but as time wears on the allowances made are fewer and more grudging, and they become progressively more isolated and excluded from society.

People who fail to make a return for the things they receive are isolated and rejected. Some sociologists have represented this as another sort of exchange – the exchange of support for status. All social services, Bob Pinker writes, are an exchange of service for status. All of them, consequently, carry a stigma.[163]

A culture of dependency?

Let's go on to the core of the argument, that poor people are trapped in dependency. Once they have tasted the fruits of poor relief, the argument runs, they are unable to wean themselves off it. There are reasons to hesitate about the statement. Benefit systems are complex, and the circumstances that people find themselves in are fairly varied. In most of Europe, people who are receiving basic social assistance benefits fall into four main categories. These are older people, unemployed people (see Box 9), single parents and people with chronic sickness or disabilities. (There may be other entitled groups – for example, widows and people leaving care – and further sub-classifications are possible, but this is close enough for present purposes.)

Of the four groups, the main group which fits the general statement that poor people are dependent, is older people. Older people on low incomes are unlikely to move to better incomes, they receive benefits in the long term, and their income is substantially provided by systems of social protection, often provided by the state. The position of older people in retirement has been referred to as 'structural dependency'[164]; dependency is both legitimate and, to a large degree, expected of older people.

Disabled people also have limited movement on and off benefit, though because many disabled people have the capacity to work, there may be movement when there is a high demand for labour. There is an overlap between disability and retirement, in two ways. The first is that most disabled people tend to be older. This holds true even within the cohort of people of working age: for example, stroke is principally experienced by people over the age of 65, but it is still one of the main causes of disability in the 45- to 65-year-old age group.[165] The second reason for overlap is that illness is a major reason for early retirement. In circumstances where people with failing health might legitimately be classified as disabled, incapacitated or unemployed, the conditions of benefit receipt have a major influence in deciding how they will be classified, and so whether or not they are subsequently considered capable of returning to the labour market.[166]

The other two groups relate to the issue of 'dependency' much less directly. Most people who are unemployed are unemployed for relatively short periods of time, but unemployment is a reverse queue, where the last to become unemployed are the most likely to exit from unemployment. The numbers of long-term unemployed people who receive benefits tend to be a low proportion of the total figures. In the case of single parents, the turn-round is slower. Single parenthood comes to an end in two main ways: one where the single parent remarries, the other where children cease to be part of the household. Single parents may also cease to be on benefits if they get work, and that tends to happen more as the children are older. This means that the typical length of time on benefits as a single parent after divorce or the birth of a child is unlikely to stretch beyond a few years.

Overall, this means that, with the main exception of older people and a smaller number of disabled people, long-term dependent poverty is relatively unusual. Research on the dynamics of benefit receipt finds that people move on and off benefit rolls with varying frequency.[167] Many people are likely to go through periods on low incomes, of different lengths: the figures for Britain suggest that, in the period 1991-2003, most of the population fell below the threshold for at least one year; only 1% fell below it for all 13 years.[168] The primary use of benefits for people of working age is not long-term support, but income maintenance in the short-to-medium term. European systems are generally referred to as 'social protection'. That is what benefits do; they protect people. They tide them over when they are in need. When they cease being in need, they go to work, and contribute to the system in their turn.

The last part of the argument is that poor people have adjusted their attitudes and behaviour to form a culture of dependency. The main contemporary advocate of this idea is Lawrence Mead. Mead argues that the underclass 'are distinctive not in their beliefs but in their inability to conform to them as closely as other people'.[169]

> More important than any economic factor as a cause of poverty, I believe, is what used to be called the culture of poverty. Surveys and ethnographic studies suggest that poor adults want to work and observe other mainstream values. Many, however, resist taking the low paid jobs that are most likely to be available to them. A greater number are simply defeatist. ... This element has given rise to much of the underclass.[170]

The circumstances that people in the 'underclass' find themselves in lead them to form different attitudes and approaches. These views are transmitted through families and neighbourhoods. Mead argues for a firm, moralistic response. The main criticism made of his analysis is a structural one: the reason, his critics argue, that people are not taking jobs is not a difference in views, but that there are no jobs available.[171]

Benefits for poor people

Whether or not people are able to 'depend' on social security benefits depends on the rules of the benefits. The structure of social security schemes is a difficult subject in its own right, and in a book of this kind it is only possible to scratch the surface. Social security is often identified in English-speaking countries with support for the poor; that reflects the influence of the English Poor Law, the first state system. But social security is not only aimed at the poor, and in some countries, some provisions like pensions are mainly the province of the better off, and not available to poor people at all.

Box 9: Unemployment

Table 9.1 shows average unemployment rates in selected European countries.[172] Figures on employment make most sense in relation to developed economies, because there has to be a functioning formal economy before the idea of 'employment' and 'unemployment' are properly applicable. Even then, there are considerable differences in the way that unemployment figures are collected. Whether people are 'unemployed' depends on whether they are seeking work; definitions of disability, single parenthood and early retirement can be interpreted to leave out people in a wide range of circumstances. The International Labour Organization treats 'unemployed' people as those who are out of work, available to start work in the next two weeks, and who have actively sought work during the last four weeks. Typically, women are treated as 'unemployed' only if they have some record of previous employment or some entitlement to benefits, and sometimes not even then. Selecting the figures for men in Table 9.1 emphasises the difference in the way nations count unemployment – any similar discrepancy among women might have been plausibly explained by differential rates of participation in the labour market.

Table 9.1: Male employment and unemployment in some European countries

Country	Male employment (% of men aged 15-64)	Male unemployment (% of labour force)
Sweden	74.6	6.4
Netherlands	79.9	4.3
UK	77.3	5.4
France	69	8.3
Germany	71.1	8.2
Austria	75.1	4.9
Denmark	80.1	3.8
Spain	75	6.6

The figures show some discrepancies between the ratio of men who are employed and those who are counted as unemployed. Austria and Spain have virtually the same proportion of employed men, but they have different unemployment figures. France and Germany have very similar male unemployment rates, but Germany employs substantially more men. The differences are partly accounted for by differences in education and retirement age. (Unemployment can fall if people are moved to early retirement, stay on at school or college, put in prison, and the like, but labour force participation will not increase, and the financial cost associated with unemployment will not be reduced.) There are more complexities in unemployment figures than I have considered here – the rates for female employment raise many more difficult issues – but the general point is still sound: non-employment, or non-participation in the labour market, is regarded differently according to the conventions of the country where it happens. In some countries it is accepted, or 'institutionalised'; in others, it is not.

There are many different approaches to supporting poor people with benefits. One of the main conceptual distinctions lies between 'universality' and 'selectivity'. Selective benefits are aimed (or 'targeted') at the poor and only at the poor. The key element in selectivity is not just that benefits are meant to go to poor people, but that they exclude other people who are not poor. This means that there has to be a test of some sort. The usual way of separating poor people from non-poor people is a 'means test', which is at root a test of income. People above a certain income do not qualify, and people below that income level do. There are many variations. Some benefits have tests of capital and resources; some have more complicated formulas, allowing for people to retain more income above the minimum threshold; some have moral conditions attached, so they are not available, for example, to people who are expected to be independent, like the non-disabled unemployed male. There are also some benefits based on different kinds of test: the Poor Law used the 'workhouse test' to check that people were both destitute and desperate before they could receive help.

There are, however, many problems with means tests. Some are intrinsic to means testing: income fluctuates, it is difficult to establish, and measuring it leads to peculiar inequities between people with monetary and non-monetary resources. Some are generally true of any benefit which tries to identify people's needs: tests are complex and expensive to administer, there are always boundary problems in deciding who qualifies and who does not, and there are problems at the points where people cease to be entitled. Selective benefits of all kinds have similar failings, and they often fail to reach the people who are entitled to them.

The main alternatives to selective benefits are 'universal' benefits. Universal benefits are nominally available to everyone, though that is not really how they work; rather, they are aimed at everyone in a broad category of people, like Child Benefit in the UK or the Citizens' Pension in New Zealand. Universal benefits help people who are poor by helping everyone in a category, meeting the needs of poor people along with others. This has two main advantages: it is easier to administer, and it is less likely to have the problems of take-up. The main disadvantage is that, inevitably, dealing with a much larger group of people is more expensive, and universal benefits tend either to be costly or to be offered at a relatively low level.

The debate between universality and selectivity has been revived in recent years in debates on 'targeting', which is treated on both sides as a synonym for selectivity. Targeting actually means something different. It is about getting benefits to the target group, who may or may not be poor – it is just as possible to target other types of group, like students, farmers or civil servants. There is a growing literature on targeting which is not about means testing.[173] Developing countries may want to help people who are poor, but they do not necessarily have the administrative capacity to conduct tests on individuals or households to see who is poor and who is not. It is possible, for example, to pick out the kinds of foods that poor people are more likely to eat, and to subsidise those foods, as a way of helping poor people.[174] Means testing does get resources to poor people, but so do some other measures in developing countries, including picking out poor areas and programmes aimed at getting people into work. By contrast, programmes which have relied on communities to come up with bids, and those which have targeted older people, have tended to be less effective, and have favoured the better off.[175]

Developed economies have mainly gone down another route, building up systems of social protection from a mix of universal, selective and insurance-based benefits. In most of Europe, benefits are mainly insurance-based, depending on contributions from people in work, with extra benefits for people who are left out. The coverage of this kind of system is patchy, and the move to 'social inclusion' has been concerned to make these systems more comprehensive.

TEN

Poverty and politics

The social position of poor people is often identified in terms of inequality – the things that poor people do not have, and others do. Richer people are able to take certain things for granted: that they have the rights, freedoms and status of every other citizen. Poor people do not have the same assurance. Obviously, many of the world's poorest people live in societies that are not democracies, and political inequality goes hand in hand with other forms of disadvantage. But it is also true in the world's rich democracies that poor people are likely to be those who lack the rights which everyone else has.

The first, and most fundamental, of those rights, is freedom. Freedom is conventionally understood in terms of 'negative' and 'positive' concepts. A 'negative' idea of freedom says that people are free when they are not being constrained or coerced by other people. A 'positive' view says that people are poor if they do not have the power to act. People who are poor are obviously not free in the positive sense. Several critics have argued forcefully that the negative sense is the only valid view, and that it does not relate to poverty. Isaiah Berlin, for example, suggests:

> It is argued, very plausibly, that if a man is too poor to afford something on which there is no legal ban – a loaf of bread, a journey round the world, resource to the law courts – he is as little free to have it as he would be if it were forbidden him by law. ... If my poverty were a kind of disease, which prevented me from buying bread ... as lameness prevents me from running, this inability would not naturally be described as a lack of freedom. [176]

Poverty, to Berlin, could only be considered an infringement of freedom if it was held to result from the actions of others.[177] But, even within this narrow understanding of freedom, there are at least two other ways in which poverty could be thought of as a limitation on freedom. The first is that poverty limits opportunities, and in circumstances where people do not have choices, any limitation or constraint is likely to lead to coercion. If someone has ten roads to follow, and one is closed, that person still has nine. If he only has two, and one is closed, he no longer has any choice about where to go. Poor people lack choices in many of the essentials of life – housing, schooling and work opportunities. In the terms of a negative view of freedom, poverty may not limit freedom, but it certainly makes people vulnerable, and it limits their choices. To take a small example, many countries prevent the sale of body parts, such as kidneys or lungs.

The people who might be persuaded to sell their body parts are people who are constrained by poverty. The existing trade is characterised by exploitation, but beyond that it implies further, often permanent, restriction of the capacities of poor people, a choice they make because their options are so limited.

The second problem is that, when people are poor enough, they can have no choices at all. Jeremy Waldron gives a graphic picture of the position of homeless single people in the US. They find themselves in a limbo, where they have nowhere to sleep, nowhere to sit, nowhere to wash, and nowhere to go to the toilet. If they try to do these things, they can be ejected or arrested. They are poor, and they are being coerced by other people because of their poverty.[178]

There seems to be little reason, even so, why we should accept such a limited view of freedom.[179] All freedom, Maccallum suggests, has three elements. Freedom is freedom of a person, from constraint, to do something.[180] If people are not free to do things, they are not free at all. Poor people are people who are not able to do things – possibly because they lack the resources, possibly because they do not have the things they need to live, possibly because they are socially excluded. 'It is not the poverty of my people that appals me', Aneurin Bevan once said, 'it is the poverty of their choice.' One of the fundamental moral arguments for responding to poverty is an argument about the value of personal freedom. If you believe that people should be free, and able to make choices, you believe that they should not be poor.

Power and empowerment

Poor people lack power in several ways. Where they lack economic resources, the choices they can make are circumscribed by other people. Where they are socially excluded, they lack influence and the capacity that comes from social connections and networks. And where they are in need, they have to devote their efforts and attention to meeting those needs. 'Power' is often represented in conspiratorial terms, as if decisions were made by a small number of extremely privileged people, but it does not need to be. People have power over their lives if they are able to control the events that affect them. And they lack power when they cannot.

It is not necessarily true, however, that poor people have no power. In the first place, there are large variations in the condition of people who are poor. In part, this reflects the wide range of definitions of poverty, but it also results from the wide range of conditions that poor people are found in; the influence and networks of an older person on a limited income is very different from an unemployed teenager. Second, there are different sorts of power, exercised in different spheres. People can have social, economic or political power. People can have legal rights or political influence even where they do not have social or economic power. Third, people may still have the formal rights of citizenship. Because poor people have the vote in western society, they have some level of political influence. This can seem minimal, but if Amartya Sen is right it is one of the crucial differences between societies where people are desperately poor and those where poor people receive social protection.[181]

The idea of 'empowerment' has taken root mainly as a way of talking about disadvantaged groups – for example, women (see Box 10), people in excluded minorities, disabled people, and of course people in poor communities. It has been one of the motivating principles behind participatory research for people who are poor – 'less a method', Lister comments, 'than a philosophy'.[182]

Box 10: Gender and empowerment

The World Bank describes poverty in terms of opportunity, capability, security and empowerment.[183] The disadvantage of women makes them vulnerable to poverty in all of these respects. The main indicators chosen to represent disadvantage are concerned with education, literacy, participation in the labour market, and political engagement. (Although these correspond to opportunity, capability, security and empowerment, the factors are not genuinely distinct: each is rooted in a more general experience of disadvantage.)

Education. The UN committed itself to eliminating gender disparity in primary and secondary education, preferably by 2005, and in all levels of education no later than 2015. However, 2005 has come and gone, and there are still serious inequalities in access to primary education. In South Asia 61% of girls, and 86% of boys, finish primary education.[184]

Literacy. In most developing countries where records are kept, women's literacy is not greatly different from men's. There is parity in Latin America and some Middle Eastern countries, including Jordan and Iran. However, in other countries, notably in Africa and South Asia, fewer women are able to read: the ratio is 0.9 in Algeria, 0.8 in India and 0.6 in Pakistan.[185]

Participation in the labour market. Women are much less likely than men to participate in the labour market, and consequently much less likely to have an independent income. The ratios range from 0.2 to 0.3 in some Arab countries (Iraq, Saudi Arabia and the Gulf States) to relative equality in some African and South-East Asian countries (Ghana, Burundi, Malawi and Vietnam). Cambodia has more women employed than men. In developed economies the ratio tends to be between 0.6 and 0.8.[186]

Political participation. The World Bank uses a crude indicator of political participation, which is the proportion of women at ministerial level. This ranges from zero to 20%, with only six countries listed with a higher proportion than 20%. The highest proportion is in Denmark, with 41% of female ministers.[187]

Empowerment is used in two main senses – individual and collective. Individually, empowerment is about protecting the position of each and every person. The kinds of measure which have been used have been based partly in individual rights, including constitutional protection and legal remedies. Collectively, empowerment is about making structures for groups and communities to take control of their situation, through collective action, including political organisation and attempts to give people a voice.

Entitlement

If poor people lack power, they lack rights; they do not have the means to control their lives or bring about positive change. Sen has taken this a stage further. He argues not simply that people in poverty lack rights, but that their poverty has to be understood in terms of the lack of rights.[188]

The core of this argument rests in Sen's work on famine. Most people before Sen would have assumed that the reason for famine was that there is not enough food to eat. Poor people suffer disproportionately, because when there is a competition for scarce resources, their poverty means that they will lose it. Sen's work shows, startlingly, that this is not what is actually happening. In every case of famine he has looked at, there has been enough food. For example, in the Irish famine of the 1840s, Ireland continued to export food; the starving people on the hillsides had to watch boatloads of food being shipped out to market in England.[189] The central issue in famine is not that food is short; it is that poor people are not allowed to eat the food which is there.

Famines happen for many reasons: for example, one of the common problems linked with famine is civil war, which cuts food supplies off to part of the population. The situation is rarely quite so clear cut as the Irish case. But this is still a deeply disturbing finding. The central point remains, that there would be enough food if only it was distributed differently. That is the root of Sen's argument that poverty consists mainly of a lack of entitlement. In the economic market, this means that people do not have economic resources. In social and political terms, it may mean that they are unable to exercise the power and influence that they need to bring resources to them. Another striking observation made by Sen is the assertion that there has never been a famine in a democracy. There are problems of definition here – for example, India would have claimed to have been a democracy by the time of the famine of the 1950s (and it still has major problems of child malnutrition), and the countries currently threatened by famine in East Africa have various political systems – but the association is worth thinking about. Is the issue that democracy depends on countries being rich enough, and peaceable enough, to avoid major problems: or is there something about democracy which leads to poor people being given more rights? Sen thinks it is the latter. The institutions of democracy – voting, economic exchange and a press which is able to bring the government to account – all help to give poor people the rights they might otherwise be denied. Sen's arguments have been profoundly influential in international organisations, where poverty is interpreted increasingly in terms of a lack of rights, and responses to poverty are coming to take the form of a declaration of rights.

The rights of the poor

Rights are rules which govern social relationships. Poor people can be protected by other sorts of rule: in mediaeval times, the main protection they had was an appeal to charity. The duties that led people to charities were understood as duties to God, rather than to poor people. Rights are different, because they are held, and can be insisted on, by the people they protect.

There are several kinds of rights, and they mean different things. First, there is a distinction between rights which give duties to other people, or 'claim rights', and liberties. In developed countries, we tend to assume that poor people have the same liberties accorded to others, and debates about protection of the poor consequently focus on claim rights. The liberties cannot be taken for granted, as the example of homeless people shows, but the argument is not without substance. The main problems stem not so much from deliberate restriction as from the lack of choice; liberty is important, but it is not enough, and poor people need claim rights to be able to exercise choice. In developing countries, poor people also lack liberty. The problem is not just that poor people do not have the resources to live; they are often prevented from the kind of security which would make it possible for them to get those resources. A recurring problem in *Voices of the poor* is abuse of authority, particularly by the police.[190]

A second key distinction lies between particular and general rights. Particular rights depend on the unique circumstances of each person. Social security in most of Europe is based on personal rights, such as pensions, unemployment assistance and medical care which are geared to a person's work record. Relatively little is given to broad categories of people, like people on low incomes. General rights are categorical; they go to everyone in a broad group, like children or older people. These rights have been beneficial for poor people, but they also tend to be limited in their scope, and in the amount they give.

The third key distinction is between moral and legal rights. The term 'welfare rights' is mainly used to refer to legal rights to social protection. The main test of legal rights is the ability to enforce them, through some kind of sanction. Legal rights look as if they should be more important than moral rights, but there are arguments to the contrary. The first is that where such rights are affirmed – for example, in the Universal Declaration of Human Rights, or the UN's Declaration of the Rights of the Child – they may still have a persuasive effect within key organisations, both national and international. Second, in cases where legal rights exist but are not approved morally, there may be problems in enforcing the rights. 'Where morality is at issue', Joel Handler argues, 'welfare is conditioned, regardless of any notional entitlement'.[191] By contrast, legal rights which are ill-defined but morally approved of, like the rights of people to (discretionary) medical care in the UK, carry considerable weight in practice. Both moral and legal rights are important to change the social relationships of poor people.

There is sometimes the sense in discussions in international organisations that all we have to do to overcome poverty is to sprinkle it with legal rights and the problems will disappear. Clearly, there is a limit to what rights can do. They are important, not just as a symbol, but as a way of dealing with some fundamental problems. Those problems include poor people's lack of entitlement, their limited power, and the social exclusion which so often lies at the heart of the experience of poverty.

Poverty and democracy

Democratic governments have generally come to accept responsibility for poverty. Right-wing critics have tended to see this as a process of some people voting to give themselves resources belonging to other people, and a slippery slope. But a similar argument has been made about the 'middle-class hijack' of the welfare state: where most of the population receives benefits, they have a strong interest to maintain and protect their rights.[192] Most democratic countries have learned to accept social protection in general, and health care in particular, as a central part of the services they provide for their citizens. If Sen is right about the nature of entitlement, and the influence of the political process, then poverty can be prevented through the development of democratic governance. Sen attributes this to the system of government – like the process of voting, the establishment of formal opposition, or the accountability of government to the electorate. He writes:

> If the survival of a government is threatened by the prevalence of hunger, the government has an incentive to deal with the situation. ...
> In democratic countries, even very poor ones, the survival of the ruling government would be threatened by famine, since elections are not easy to win after famines; nor is it easy to withstand criticism of opposition parties and newspapers. That is why famine does not occur in democratic countries.[193]

If democracy legitimates redistribution, it does not do so directly. If one person has food in store, and ten others are starving, the ten cannot simply vote to raid the other person's store. There are states where this kind of calculation may have some influence – like the early days of Soviet Russia, or the attempts of Robert Mugabe's regime in Zimbabwe to redistribute land holding – but they are not usually thought of as 'democratic'. Despite the preconceptions of many of those who work in the Anglo-American tradition, redistribution by the state is not the characteristic mode of social protection in many countries. The 'welfare states' came relatively late to the provision of social welfare, and most were established against a background of pre-existing voluntary, independent and mutualist effort. The general commitment made by democratic states has not been to universal redistribution, but to provision in circumstances where other methods have failed.

The link between democratic institutions and poverty relief is a fairly crude version of a rather more sophisticated argument. Sen argues that famines are caused by lack of entitlement, and democracies can be said to avoid famine through the development of entitlement. Democracies create entitlements, and entitlements are the means by which poverty can be avoided. Those entitlements are manifest in economic engagement, political rights and social rights. Democracy, by this account, is about rights.

Probably the best-known rights-based model of democracy is that of liberal democracy. Liberal democracy is based partly on the principles of liberal individualism; it is also strongly influenced by the American republican tradition. The key elements were individual liberty; pluralism; and the rule of law, and its primacy over government. Some rights are widely recognised in the liberal model. They include civil rights – equality before the law, freedom of religion and freedom of assembly – and political rights, including the right to free speech, the right to vote, and the right to participate in politics. They do not commonly assume economic rights, including free exchange, employment rights or movement of labour and capital; nor do they include social rights, such as rights to Income Support, health care or housing. And yet rights of this kind, if not universal, are commonplace in democratic governments. Democracy has helped the poor, not simply through the removal of obstacles, but through the establishment of material rights and public services. The idea of 'liberal democracy' has it nearly right, but it underemphasises economic and social rights. Economic development depends on integration in economic processes, which both stems from entitlement and promotes it. Social protection develops entitlements and basic security. Democracy is a system of government which guarantees such entitlements. That is how it helps the poor.

'Government', Edmund Burke once wrote, 'is a contrivance of human wisdom to provide for human wants'.[194] Governments are accountable to their citizens, and citizens want them to do things that are useful and valued. In right-wing mythology, this mainly relates to defence and law and order, but is not everything that governments are there for. A whole clutch of new states have been formed since the 1980s, and in general their biggest priority has been not to secure defence, but to promote economic prosperity.

Promoting the interests of citizens means that governments are expected to foster economic development, promote basic security and protect the rights of their citizens. Social protection is not provided only by government – in many countries, it is not even mainly done by them – but governments generally have a role which is especially significant for poor people. The government is, by default, the provider of last resort. There are considerable variations in this role in OECD countries: some countries have a relatively wide residual safety net provision (like the UK and France), while others have partial or incomplete systems (like Germany and the US). Some people flatter their societies by thinking that families or charities will step into the breach.[195] They only do it in part. For the rest, if governments don't do it, no one else does.

It is difficult, however, for governments to stop with nothing more than a safety net.[196] There are both political problems, and practical ones. In political terms, this sort of provision is deeply resented, and is likely to be rejected as a 'public burden'. People may vote for measures they may stand to benefit from themselves; residual welfare, by contrast, is widely rejected. Even in relation to residual provision, however, people often want more; even if voters seem to disapprove of welfare in general, there are always instances of pressing need which push governments to plug the gap. In practical terms, residual welfare is expensive: it is cumbersome and difficult to administer. The boundaries are never clear; there are problems of definition, and problems of fairness. This is an issue charities and other independent organisations can live with, but governments have to account for their actions to their electorates, and they find it much more difficult to be arbitrary. Overall, because poverty affects so much in people's lives, it is difficult to hold to a single area, such as work or education, and not to step beyond the boundaries. The Poor Law, which was the first national system, began with poor relief and 'setting the poor on work'; it gradually took on extra responsibilities, such as public health, education and medical care. The general experience of governments has been that they cannot hold the line, and there is a gradual expansion of responsibilities.

Part Five
Poverty as a moral concept

ELEVEN

The moral dimensions of poverty

This part of the book tackles some controversial material. Poverty is a moral concept, as well as a descriptive one. How prominent morality is in the debate depends, to some extent, on what our understanding of 'poverty' is, but moral issues run all the way through arguments about poverty.

Why should people who are not poor accept responsibility for people who are? This is, at root, a moral question. Like most moral questions, it is not capable of being proved. Nearly all societies do, however, have some kind of arrangement for protecting people who are poor. Often this takes the form of charity, or the sense of *noblesse oblige* – that rich people have responsibilities to poorer people. This includes many tribal societies: Marshall Sahlins, an anthropologist, gives examples from more than seventy.[197]

The first argument for accepting responsibility is, simply, humanitarian. If there is no responsibility for poor people, then poor people will suffer. This is central to many moral principles, including some religious positions, and arguments based in common humanity. For practical purposes, this position is beyond argument; either one accepts it, or one does not.

The second argument is more complicated, but it probably reflects better the way that people actually feel about moral responsibility. Most people do not feel the same responsibility to everyone, regardless of circumstances. People are born into families, and into social groups. Our first duty is to our families, then to friends, then to neighbours, and so forth. The people who we have the greatest responsibility to are the people we are closest to. (The argument is almost circular – this is part of what being 'closer' means.) Someone from London will probably feel more responsibility for an older person in Bognor than a child on the street in Bogota – or, for that matter, for a migrant from other countries (see Box 11). This is the same concept as the idea of 'solidarity' found in Catholic social teaching. Solidarity is the responsibility that people have to other people around them.[198] A society is made up of a series of networks of solidarity, connected to each other.

Third, there are charitable duties. Charity is not necessarily based in any concern with the person who receives charity; it can be a duty to God, not to other people. This was the approach taken by mediaeval monasteries, before the Reformation. The model is still present in the constitution of some charities, which are set up to reflect the wishes of their founders rather than the needs of the people who may benefit from them.

Fourth, there are rights. The issues of rights were discussed in Chapter Ten. There is an argument to say that poor people do not have rights: that is why they are poor. But the converse of this is that advocates for the poor have tried to argue that the rights of the poor should be extended. The language of rights is, commonly, a way of trying to put the moral claims of the poor. This is most obvious in the arguments for human rights, which are intended to apply to every poor person irrespective of circumstances, or the reasons why they are poor. The United Nations has supported several declarations of rights, including the Universal Declaration of Human Rights, the International Covenant on Economic, Social and Cultural Rights and the UN Convention on the Rights of the Child. A draft convention on the rights of disabled people is currently being discussed.

The language of rights points in another direction. In any modern society, people gain entitlements through their engagement in economic activity. If the fourth point was concerned with general, or universal, rights, the fifth argument is based in particular rights – the rights that each person has gained. Pensions schemes, for example, are commonly based, not in a general right to everyone above a certain age, but in a set of earned rights, developed through a system of contributions, and commonly reflecting a person's work record over a long period of time. This sort of right has been hugely important in the response to poverty, and it is difficult to underestimate its moral force. If we put the question, 'why should this person be supported?', the answer may well be, 'because this person has paid for their entitlement', or that someone else has – their employer, their spouse, their parents.[199]

The same principle extends more generally through the concept of 'reciprocity'. Some reciprocity is 'balanced', when people gain entitlements through direct exchange. But other forms of reciprocity are 'generalised', so that it is difficult to tell who is at the start of the chain, and who is at the end of it.[200] People support younger generations because they were supported when they were young; they support older generations because the older generation supported people before them. 'Solidarity' is often used in Europe to refer, not just to the specific obligations that people have to others, but to the networks of reciprocity and mutual responsibility which have been developed.[201]

This understanding of solidarity falls rather short of the general obligation to poor people that is implied by humanitarianism, charity or universal human rights. It is confined, and specific. Box 11 points to the kind of issue which becomes problematic – migrants and asylum seekers – who may not benefit from networks of solidarity, because they come from outside them.

Accepting that someone is poor generally means that their situation is serious, and that something ought to be done about it. For people who do not accept moral responsibility, there are two main ways of avoiding it. One is to claim that poverty is not serious: either people are not really poor, or poverty is not so bad. This position is discussed in the next section. The other is to say that there is something else about them which excuses us from moral responsibility – the kind of person they are, the way they behave, the reason why they are poor, or why they really ought to be poor. These positions have been discussed in part in Chapters Eight and Nine, and there is more to come in Chapter Twelve.

Box 11: Migrants and asylum seekers

Although we may think of duties to humanity in general, for most people, moral obligation is structured by geography and social contact. We generally acknowledge the greatest duty to the people who are closest to us. But people from other countries don't always stay in those countries. Some are forced to escape their countries to avoid war and political conflict, as refugees or asylum seekers. Estimates of the numbers are given in Table 11.1.[202] If the issues were strictly issues of human rights, the nationality of the potential recipient cannot be the primary consideration, and people who are refugees or stateless are necessarily the responsibility of the society where they happen to be (which is the position in international law). The rejection of immigration and asylum on these terms is communitarian in form — governments intend to put their own citizens first.

Table 11.1: Refugees

Region	Number of refugees at the end of 2005
Central Africa	1,193,700
East and Horn of Africa	772,000
West Africa	377,200
Central Asia and Middle East	2,467,300
Americas	564,300
Asia and Pacific	825,600
Europe	1,965,800
Total	**8,394,500**

Many more people try to move to richer countries, as 'economic migrants', in order to improve their lives. Some are poor, but economic migrants also include people who are more skilled; the money sent back to poorer countries, known as 'remittances', has a substantial impact on the economies of the poorest countries in the world. Because people who are persecuted also commonly suffer economic restrictions, and because people on low incomes are often subject to harassment by authorities, it can be difficult to tell migrants and refugees apart.

Are people really poor?

Most social scientists working on poverty have concentrated on the question of whether people are 'really' poor. Rowntree knew that many people would deny that the people in his studies were poor. When Charles Booth had claimed that people were poor on 18 to 21 shillings per week, critics had protested that people could live on much less. Bosanquet had argued that:

> there are comparatively few families in London through whose hands there had not passed in the course of the year sufficient money and money's worth to have made a life free at any rate from hunger and cold, and with much in it of good.[203]

Rowntree tried to make his arguments proof against this kind of criticism. The approach he took was to introduce a standard of poverty that was so strict that no one could reasonably argue with it. People were in primary poverty when their income was so low that it was inconceivable that they should live on it. The test he applied was the minimum to allow for 'physical efficiency'. Rowntree described primary poverty in these terms:

> let us clearly understand what 'merely physical efficiency' means. A family living on the scale allowed for in this estimate must never spend a penny on railway fare or omnibus. They must never go into the country unless they walk. They must never purchase a halfpenny newspaper or spend a penny to buy a ticket for a popular concert. They must write no letters to absent children, for they cannot afford to pay the postage. They must never contribute anything to their church or chapel, or give any help to a neighbour which costs them money. They cannot save, nor can they join sick club or Trade Union, because they cannot pay the necessary subscriptions. The children must have no pocket money for dolls, marbles or sweets. The father must smoke no tobacco, and must drink no beer. The mother must never buy any pretty clothes for herself or for her children. ... Should a child fall ill, it must be attended by the parish doctor; should it die, it must be buried by the parish. Finally, the wage-earner must never be absent from his work for a single day. If any of these conditions are broken, the extra expenditure involved is met, and can only be met, by limiting the diet. [204]

His research in York found that nearly 10% of everyone he surveyed was in primary poverty; a further 3% were within two shillings of the line, and 8.5% more within six shillings of it. Rowntree went on to suggest that many more people were in 'secondary poverty'; they were poor, but they were above the line of primary poverty. The point of this distinction was not to judge people in secondary poverty; it was to prove that people in primary poverty were poor beyond doubt, and that they could not be condemned for mismanaging their resources. These were people who would still be poor even if they managed their affairs perfectly.

We are a century on from Rowntree, but many of the arguments are still the same. Although social scientists argue earnestly about issues of measurement and method, the core of their concerns is often something different – how to define and describe poverty in a way that will get something done about it. Issues of measurement and identification were discussed in earlier chapters, and it is not necessary to repeat that material here. We need to be aware, though, that some of the arguments about the issue have little to do with their strengths or weaknesses as descriptions of poverty. Three typical criticisms might help to give some idea of the way that debates about definition are linked with the moral arguments.

1. *The standards are shifting, so that improvements in the position of the better off lead to redefinition of the status of the poor.* This is true only if the standard is based in inequality, which most standards of poverty are not. However, the main inequality standard, the EU test of 'economic distance', does compare poor people with well-off people; it compares them with the median, who tend to be less well-off workers. The main objection here seems to be to any reference to inequality – which does have a direct effect on quality of life.

2. *If poverty is relative, poverty is not that serious.* This is a misunderstanding of the meaning of 'relative poverty'. Relativity is mainly about social norms and social relationships. Being excluded and unable to participate in society is different in different countries, but it does not cease to be serious.

3. *People won't die because they haven't got inessential items, like a television.* They won't, but they will die earlier because they're poor. The evidence on poverty and health consistently shows that poorer people have shorter lives and more illness. (It also shows, by the way, that they have worse medical care.) The lack of consumer goods is an indicator of that – not a cause, but a signal. Material indicators are pointers towards the problems: they are not the problems themselves.

We need to understand what is going on here. These arguments look as if they are about definition; it is debatable whether they really are. They are, rather, political positions about who should be included in our field of concern. (These three arguments reflect statements by politicians in the UK – respectively, Tony Blair[205], John Moore[206] and Keith Joseph[207].) They are moral positions, not just descriptive ones.

Is poverty such a bad thing?

The claim that poverty is a bad thing is circular. If it were not such a bad thing, we probably would not be talking about it as 'poverty'. No serious commentators claim that poverty is not a bad experience, but there is a strand of popular opinion which tends to be dismissive. Monks and nuns, the argument goes, are poor, and they don't have such a bad life. This misses the point. The 'vow of poverty' is more than 'voluntary simplicity': monks and nuns are supposed to share the hardship of the poor. The Dominicans, for example, 'went about their duties with great humility and lived a life of voluntary poverty, exposing themselves to innumerable dangers and sufferings, for the salvation of others'.[208] If it isn't hard, it isn't poverty.

Poverty has three common consequences. The first is that poverty is restrictive or limiting. If poverty is material, it means that people do not have the goods, resources and amenities they need, and they have to devote more of their time and attention to seeking those things. If poverty is economic, it means that people do not have the choices that other people have. If it is about social relationships, the scope of poor people's networks and contacts is reduced; they may be unable to participate at all, and may be excluded.

The second is that poverty is damaging. This is most obviously true of material deprivation – if people do not have the goods and services they need, their health will suffer. However, there are also strong links between indicators of health, such as life expectancy, and economic and social factors. Concerns have also been expressed about the impact of poverty on personal development, including education and self-fulfilment for adults.

The third consequence is that poverty lowers standards. Where people do not have the things they need, they have to manage as best they can. People have to adapt; they have to compromise. They compromise their material standards; they live in bad housing, or drink insanitary water, or eat unhealthy food. They compromise economically: they buy what they can, they take the jobs that are open to them, they juggle resources to manage. They adapt socially; the contribution they make, and the support they get, depends on their ability to maintain contact and social networks. One of the key moral issues for Victorian social reformers was the belief that poverty was undermining moral and religious education – that people who are concerned about managing to live at all find it more difficult to look up to the heavens. (There were also, admittedly, romantic fictions where the experience of poverty made for better, rounded people.[209]) The concern with moral education, though it may seem outmoded, hides a moral truth: living in poverty demands compromises, of time, family life and commitment to others.

For the most part, poverty has undesirable consequences for a society, as it does for the people in it, and it has those consequences for the same reasons. If poverty limits the capacity of its people, it also limits the capacity of the society. If it damages people, through ill health or slow development, it damages the profile and the experience of the whole society; the problems of the poor do not stop with the poor. If it forces standards down, then social norms and social capital are reduced. There is an argument, beyond this, to say that societies have interests going beyond the interests of the people who make it up. In the same way that societies have interests in defence and economic prosperity, societies have interests in the kinds of things which help to make them social – the promotion of culture, the socialisation of the population, the development of the next generation. Without these things, a society cannot survive – it ceases to be a society. It is debatable whether poverty threatens everything that matters – several societies have produced great cultural achievements despite widespread social misery – but it does not help, either. There are, on the other hand, clear instances of poverty preventing social development – most obviously, in the contemporary world, in developing countries, where governments and local organisations often lack the basic capacity to cope with the overwhelming problems they face.

Equally, poverty is damaging to an economy. Keynes argued that economic prosperity depended, as much as anything, on the level of economic activity. Limited resources mean limited demand; limited demand means limited production. There are virtuous and vicious circles. The virtuous circle is represented by economic growth; people with more resources demand more, economic production expands to respond to that demand, and people gain more resources in the process. Conversely, reduced resources imply reduced demand; lower demand leads to lower production, and lower production to lower resources.[210] Although the further reaches of Keynesianism are no longer accepted, it remains generally true that expenditure on poor people acts as an economic regulator. When economic production is going badly, increased expenditure on unemployment helps to protect the economy, by stopping the level of activity falling too far; when the economy grows, the level of support required reduces. The converse of this is, of course, that economies which fail to offer support for the poor suffer as a result; limited social protection is against a country's economic interests.

The idea that poverty is a bad thing has been resisted by some economic liberals. There are those who see poverty as useful, even desirable, for a society. Poverty is a spur to effort: the incentive to do well. It is also the consequence of inadequacy and lack of effort. If there were no poor, Spencer argues, no one would feel the need to do anything.

> The poverty of the incapable, the distresses that came upon the imprudent, the starvation of the idle, and those shoulderings aside of the weak by the strong, which leaves so many 'in shallows and in miseries', are the decrees of a large, far-seeing benevolence.[211]

Similarly, there are those who would argue that poverty is necessary to an economy, and in particular to the operation of the labour market; depressing benefits is seen as a way of creating an 'incentive to work' and stimulating the supply of labour. What these arguments have in common is an attempt to diminish the negative effects of poverty. If poverty is not a problem, it does not need to be remedied.

TWELVE

The moral condemnation
of the poor

Accepting that poverty is serious is only the first step towards accepting responsibility. The second step is to accept that something ought to be done. One of the most common strategies for denying that responsibility is the claim that poverty is the responsibility of the poor themselves. But the moral principles which lead people to accept responsibility are not, for the most part, affected or negated by the actions or behaviour of poor people. If poor people are suffering, they are not suffering less if it is their own fault. If we owe a charitable duty to God, it applies whether or not poor people are deserving. If poor people have rights, they have rights whether or not they have behaved badly. The only principle that is clearly affected by the conduct of poor people is the duty of solidarity. Solidarity changes according to the situation of each person. Blaming the poor changes the nature of the moral obligation between the people involved; it also turns poor people into something different from ourselves, and puts them at a distance.

By contrast with arguments about the seriousness of the issue, the moral condemnation of the poor gets much less academic attention. Here are some examples. The first is from Edward Banfield's book, *The unheavenly city*:

> The lower class individual lives in a slum and sees little or no reason to complain. He does not care how dirty and dilapidated his housing is either inside or out, nor does he mind the inadequacy of such public facilities as schools, parks and libraries; indeed, where such things exist he destroys them by acts of vandalism if he can.[212]

Charles Murray associates the underclass with 'drugs, crime, illegitimacy, homelessness, drop-out from the job market, drop-out from school and casual violence'.[213] (The literature from the US, where the government has not made the most favourable provision for the poor, still tends to be locked in the idea that provision is a public burden.) A recent report from South Africa comments:

> The government has ordered an urgent countrywide study of 14000 households to determine whether women are having babies to cash in on child-support grants. ... In a report in the *Herald* on Tuesday, a Port Elizabeth social worker alleged that many young mothers were 'generally corrupt' and deliberately fell pregnant 'to benefit themselves'.[214]

It is difficult to know how to deal with this kind of material. Looking at the arguments seriously seems to dignify them as something that is worthy of attention, and a long series of social scientists have refused to engage in the mud-slinging, arguing that since the material has no foundation at all, it is not worth talking about. The problem with this is that the arguments keep coming back; they are not going to go away because we ignore them. Many, admittedly, are 'zombie' arguments: no matter how many times they are shot down in flames or have a stake driven through their heart, they seem to get up again afterwards and keep coming. That does not mean that we should lie down and let the zombies win.

The behaviour of poor people

A central part of the moral condemnation of the poor is the idea that poor people behave badly. It is possible to argue either that poor people choose to behave differently – which makes it possible to judge the actions in moral terms – or that they are pushed into acting differently, which still makes it possible to condemn the action while trying to excuse the actor. Both positions make commentators uncomfortable. Some try to counter by pointing to the positive characteristics of the poor[215] – which falls into the trap of accepting the legitimacy of moral judgements. Others try to avoid any description relating to behaviour.

There are three main ways in which poverty might be thought to affect individual behaviour. One is the view that people do things differently when they are poor. This is fairly self-evident; if poverty means, as Townsend argues, that people who are poor lack the diets, amenities, opportunities and scope for participation in society that others have[216], then of course they behave differently – that is part of what poverty is. People who are poor don't do the things that other people do, because they can't afford them. Poor people eat differently, for example, because they cannot afford the same diet as others. It's almost a trivial point, though it becomes important in circumstances where people are blamed for the conditions they live in. Of course people who live in slums have to accept low living standards; that does not mean that they choose them. Accusations that people who live in slums have low standards can have unfortunate effects when they are used as an objection to improving housing standards for people from slum areas. Likewise, people who are poor might be accused of lack of thrift. It's true; many poor people do not save anything. This is generally because they do not have any money to save. The only odd thing about this statement is that people believe it somehow reflects on the morality of people who are poor.

The second main argument that people behave differently is that their poverty is seen as the result of their choices. People become poor when they make bad choices – typically, choices about work and childbearing. Charles Murray's book *Losing ground* uses a 'rational choice' model to argue that poor people's choices trap them in poverty. Part of this argument is based in the peculiarity of social assistance in the US, which relies heavily on a means-tested safety net, but a lot of it would have been familiar to the 19th-century liberals who criticised the Poor Law. Murray's argument is, at root, that people will not work if they are paid for doing nothing. He writes:

1. People respond to incentives and disincentives. Sticks and carrots work.
2. People are not inherently hard working or moral. In the absence of countervailing influences, people will avoid work and be amoral.
3. People must be held responsible for their actions ... [217]

This is based as much on a fundamental misunderstanding of economic incentives as on misunderstandings about poverty. People do not respond automatically to sticks and carrots, and nothing in economic theory says that they do. Economics works primarily by looking at people's behaviour on average. People's responsiveness to different issues is described in terms of 'elasticity', and the extent to which they respond varies according to their preferences and the nature of the issue. The argument about whether poor people have an incentive to work depends, in the first place, on what they stand to gain. The short answer to that is 'money', but there are other things that people get from work – status, activity, social contact, a sense of purpose, and the ability to fulfil themselves. (These factors help to explain why millions of people who do not need the money take unpaid work, like voluntary work.) People would choose not to work only if those things did not apply. The idea that people choose not to work simply because benefits exist has no basis in economic theory.

Equally misconceived is Murray's assertion that this applies 'in the absence of countervailing influences'. 'Harold' and 'Phyllis', his ideally rational couple, seem to have dropped off a passing spaceship. Real people are born into a family, a society and a community. They grow up in families, they go to school, and they learn social values. The world of work is highly socialised; there are few jobs left in the world which are not highly interdependent on the work of other people. (Most of the people to whom this does not apply, like subsistence farmers in developing countries, are very poor.) Benefits are available only in the more developed countries, and they are hemmed in by rules and conditions. Tony Atkinson points to five common assumptions in the economic literature: none of them is true.

a) the benefit is paid irrespective of the reasons for entry into unemployment
b) there are no contribution conditions related to past employment
c) the benefit is not related to past earnings in employment, and is usually assumed to be a constant flat-rate amount
d) the benefit is paid independently of the recipient's efforts to search for new work, or of availability for work
e) the benefit is paid for an unlimited duration.[218]

The common assertions that people are freely able to claim benefit instead of working, that they will be better off or nearly better off, and that they will consequently choose not to work, are generally wrong. They have no more foundation in experience than they do in theory.

Moral arguments start to gather weight only if one accepts at the outset that there is something about the poor which is worthy of condemnation. This depends on them having some moral responsibility, and something which makes them behave differently to others. The third main argument that poverty affects behaviour is that it induces a change in the psychology of the poor person. A lot of this material comes from discussions of the 'culture of poverty'[219], which will be referred to again in Chapter Thirteen, but this is really a misnomer. What arguments on the 'culture of poverty' seem to be about is not a culture, but a common set of psychological responses.

It is not wholly implausible to argue that a shared experience of deprivation promotes a widespread response. It is well established that long-term unemployment may lead to lethargy and despair[220] – which is not to say that all unemployed people react in the same way, but that the reaction may justifiably be attributed to the experience of unemployment. Haggstrom suggests that the traits of a culture of poverty describe a psychology, not of poverty, but of the 'powerlessness of poverty'[221]: a feeling of powerlessness that leads to fatalism, or taking pleasures when they come. There is an obvious problem, however, in trying to claim that any population shares common psychological traits. More than half the world's population is poor, and in developed countries estimates range from about one in twelve at the low end to one in four at the upper end, with many other people passing through poverty during stages of their lives. It makes sense to say that poor people cannot do some things, because their poverty stops them; it does not make sense to say that they all do the same thing. There comes a point at which the claim that these people think and act in the same way begins to look silly.

Situational factors

Poor people are sometimes thought to behave differently because of the circumstances they are in. They adapt to circumstances. This category of description has often been based in identification of the 'underclass' with an urban poor, as a spatial category. There are poor urban areas in most countries, including the UK and the US, where social problems are particularly evident. One definition of the 'underclass' applied in policy in the US runs as follows:

> people who live in neighbourhoods where welfare dependency, female-headed families, male joblessness and dropping out of high school are all common occurrences.[222]

Although this may be associated with some kind of class or subculture, it does not need to be. The central issue is not that people share a set of problems, but that people with a wide range of different problems live next to each other. Areas can be poor, even if some of the people who live in them are not. There are greater concentrations of poor people in certain places than in others. The process by which poor people come to live in poor areas is straightforward enough. People live where they can afford to live; if they can afford better, they move out, and if they cannot they have to accept accommodation in deprived areas.

The result is a concentration of problems in certain urban locations. There are, for example, strong correlations in the distribution of unemployment, single parenthood, juvenile crime and low social class.[223] There is also an apparent association between poor areas and mental ill health[224], though here it seems that there may be a causal link; Platt et al record that 'the reasonably firm conclusion from a vast literature is that the causal link goes from unemployment to financial strain and poor mental health and not vice versa'.[225]

This helps to explain something about the constellation of factors which lead the right wing to associate poverty with social problems. The factors Auletta, Murray and Mead attribute to the underclass[226] include some issues – welfare dependency, homelessness and marginality in the job market – which are clearly a part of the experience of poverty. People in these circumstances live near each other because poor people live near each other. There are other cases, including dropping out from school and drugs, where the relationship is more complex – they could be causes or effects of poverty – but in any case, the effect of poverty is to concentrate the problems spatially.

The main issues which are left out by such an explanation concern crime and violence. Area-based figures seem to show not so much that people in poor areas commit more crime (though that may be true[227]), but rather that they are more vulnerable to it. Downes identifies three main processes from the research. The first is that the social context of the community, including issues such as unemployment, housing density and the disruption of family and friendship networks, affects the risks of victimisation. Second, there is a strong link between arrest rates and low-quality jobs for young people. Third, the experience of being on the street – whether through truancy, unemployment or lack of social alternatives – itself greatly increases the likelihood of delinquency.[228] This seems to imply a combination of factors, relating to ecology, culture and social context.

Structural explanations for behaviour

Many of the issues which have been discussed here can be understood in structural terms. Structural explanations mean that there is something about people's situation and social circumstances which conditions their actions. We should not be surprised, for example, to discover that poor people tend to live in inferior housing. Housing is primarily distributed through the economic market, and over time people with more resources are better able to get better housing, while people with less get worse, less desirable housing. Wherever housing is in short supply, the people who are least able to choose are likely to have unsatisfactory housing, or even no housing at all. Unsurprisingly, then, poor people are more likely to be homeless; they are more likely to live in overcrowded or insanitary conditions; and they are more likely to live in higher-density housing. This is a simple matter of basic economics, and it hardly seems necessary to look for further explanations. Despite this, it is fairly commonplace to find people criticising homeless people for their lack of personal competence, their lack of life skills, and their undesirable personal habits.[229] People who live in overcrowded conditions are assumed to choose to live that way.[230] People who live in slums are assumed to be insanitary[231], as opposed to living in insanitary homes. And because people who live in high-density housing have large numbers of neighbours, the problems of having lots of people nearby – typically noise, litter and vandalism from children – are blamed on the residents.[232]

Some writers tend to respond to this sort of accusation with the assumption that poor people are not really any different from anyone else. This position has some points in its favour. There are so many poor people, in such different circumstances, that generalisations are hard to sustain. At the same time, the strategy of waving the negative comments aside has not worked very well. People can see the evidence of social problems, like crime, teenage parenthood (see Box 13) and family breakdown, and these issues are more likely to affect people who are poorer. Pretending that this does not happen does not do anyone any favours. There are good structural reasons why these things should happen.

The first issue, which is crime, was mentioned in the previous section. Poor people tend to be the victims of crime and they attract greater attention from the police. (The role of the police as part of the problems of poor people is described, at some length, in *Voices of the poor*.) In *Recession, crime and punishment*, Steven Box reviews the evidence on crime, unemployment and inequality. He argues that:

> every study to date on income inequality and property offences or non-fatal violence shows that there is a statistical, maybe even a causal, relationship.[233]

Norman Dennis argues, against this position, that crime has increased even when inequality has improved. The problem of rising crime, according to Dennis, is the 'de-moralisation' of society, the weakening of family life and the consequent loss of moral restraint.[234] There are arguments to say that this is, itself, the product of economic change.

The second trend is family breakdown. There are clear associations between poverty, single parenthood and economic marginality. Relationships between men and women are more precarious. There are strong links between marital dissolution and unemployment, whether the unemployment precedes the marriage or happens during the marriage. Cohabiting parents are likely to be on very low incomes, and cohabiting fathers are particularly likely to have been unemployed.[235] Over time, it seems that the economic pressure results in a pattern of behaviour which is different from the social norm.

Box 12: Teenage pregnancy

Despite impressions to the contrary, the numbers of teenage parents in developed economies are not growing; they are shrinking. That is the problem. Throughout most of the world, birth rates are falling. There are many reasons for this, but they include
- the changing role of women
- the economic effect of female employment, which leads to a loss of income if women leave the labour market to have children
- increasing education
- later marriage and
- the availability of contraception.

Teenage mothers are a residuum – those who have not been affected by these social changes in the same way as others. Teenage pregnancy occurs across social classes. Because abortion is widely available, many girls choose to have abortions instead.[236] Teenage motherhood, by contrast, is much less widespread. The decision to carry a child mainly depends on a positive choice, when the girl feels that it is the best option available to her; the main counterbalancing considerations are employment, education and the existence of other opportunities for personal development. That is why teenage motherhood is so much more prevalent among poorer women. The women say that the best thing they could do is to become a mother, and since they are pregnant, they may as well have the baby now as later.[237] Some governments find this impossible to believe, but it makes perfectly good sense, both economically and socially.

This is coupled with another trend, which is the likelihood that a young mother will have a child and not marry the father. This, like family breakdown, probably reflects strong economic pressures. In situations where men are economically marginal, it is probably not in the woman's interests to commit herself to the child's biological father. Jarrett quotes some African American single parents:

'Right today I'm right glad I did not marry him because he still ain't got no job.'
'If we get married and he's working, then he lose his job, I'm going to stand by him and everything. I don't want to marry nobody that don't have nothing going for themselves.... I could do bad by myself.'
'I got to see a place where he's helping me. But if you don't help, I got no time.'[238]

Condemning the poor

It must be true that there are differences in the behaviour of poor people and other people. That is part of what poverty means. It is not clear, though, that poor people choose to be different or that they are responsible for the differences. Even if they are responsible, there is nothing in this to suggest that the problems of poverty are proportionate to their fault, or that poor people generally deserve to be poor.

The strength of the moral condemnation of the poor goes rather beyond anything justified by these differences, and that suggests that what is going on is something else. Poor people are not being condemned because of their differences. The common accusations of immorality, dishonesty and dirt have been associated with poverty since time immemorial. Teenage pregnancy and scrounging on benefits are simply a dressed-up modern version of the same arguments. This position kissed reason good night a long time ago. When people are looking for justification of their prejudices, they throw in material about people's behaviour by way of justification. For the same reason, some readers and reviewers of this chapter will probably reject the arguments of this chapter vehemently. No one likes being told that they are in the grip of an emotional delusion, and if they are, it only makes things worse.

Part Six
Explanations for poverty

THIRTEEN

Why people are poor

There are six main classes of explanation as to why people become poor. The explanations are not exclusive – people can hold to more than one view at the same time – but they are sufficiently distinct to be discussed separately.

- *Pathological explanations* explain poverty in terms of the character, circumstances or behaviour of poor people themselves.
- *Familial explanations* see poverty as the result of family background, genetics, inheritance and the influence of the family.
- *Sub-cultural explanations* see poverty in terms of the culture, attitudes or behaviour of a group of people, such as a neighbourhood, racial or religious group.
- *Resource-based explanations*. If there are not enough resources to go round, someone, somewhere will be poor.
- *Structural explanations*. Poverty is seen as the result of social structures or organisation, such as class, the organisation of the economy and social divisions.
- *Agency explanations*. Explanations based on external agency see poverty as the fault of someone or something – government, private firms, or agencies – who ought to have dealt with poverty and have not done so.

Pathological explanations

The idea that poverty is the fault of the poor themselves is deeply entrenched. Poverty is sometimes represented in terms of personal character or ability. People compete for resources, and people who are less able to compete – for example, people who have learning disabilities, people with mental problems and physically disabled people – are likely to lose out in the competition. Some people think this process is desirable. That legitimates disadvantage, but it would not justify poverty. Disadvantage only leads to poverty when it is so severe that it leads to people being excluded, or unable to participate in society. The quick answer is, then, that there needs to be some way of including people who are disadvantaged, rather than penalising them.

A second pathological view is that poor people are poor because of their own actions – because of the choices they make or the way they behave. An example often given in contemporary debates is the position of the unmarried teenage mother. A girl who has a child without the support of a father is likely to be trapped in poverty for some time, and the circumstance is one of the main predictors of poverty among young women and children in developed countries. The interpretation is questionable, but the argument obviously appeals to many commentators on poverty. It is backed up by strong moral condemnation of the poor.

Familial explanations

Some explanations for poverty focus on the family background or inheritance of the poor person. One example is genetic, or biological: the argument that it is in the nature of poor people to be so. This idea has a long pedigree, currently draped in the pseudo-science of geneticists who announce the discovery of genes for every human characteristic – characteristics like gambling, alcoholism or intelligence – with depressing regularity. One of the most notorious recent examples is presented in *The bell curve*, which identifies intelligence with 'race' in the US.[239] Educational attainment, career prospects and performance in tests are all conditioned by the society that people grow up in. We know that African Americans are relatively disadvantaged; what is offensive is the suggestion that this is because of their intrinsic inferiority.

Transmission in families does not need a biological explanation, however. We can see why people might assume that deprivation runs in families. People generally grow up with their families, and where they cannot, social care agencies try their best to match people's background, ethnicity and religion. Where people are disadvantaged, their families are also disadvantaged. There is nothing surprising about the idea that an unemployed father might have an unemployed teenage son: unemployment is often indicative of disadvantage, they live in the same household, they are part of the same local economy.

An example of this is the idea of the 'cycle of deprivation', put by Sir Keith Joseph in the 1970s. Poor people, he suggested, have poor children, who grow up to be poor in their turn. Joseph, much to his credit, set up research to find out what happened and how. The working party of transmitted deprivation, one of the largest social science projects of its kind, showed comprehensively that the argument was untrue, and why.[240] Job opportunities, location and partners make big differences to people's lives. Most research on the dynamics of poverty shows that most poor people cease to be poor after a relatively short period of time. The same applies to their children. Children have two main chances of escaping poverty, which are through work and marriage: poor people who marry non-poor people usually cease to be poor. In each generation, then, there is considerable movement, and a reduction in the original group of people identified as poor. A major longitudinal study was incorporated into Joseph's research programme; it covered 40 years, from 1950 to 1990, of selected families in Newcastle upon Tyne in the UK. In that time, most poor people worked, and many married out of poverty. Any generational effects had largely disappeared after two generations.[241]

One study reports extraordinarily high figures for intergenerational continuity: 26% of poor African American children were poor as adults.[242] That is remarkably high, but it still means that 74% are not poor as adults. If the trend continues, 7% will be poor after two generations, 2% after three, and one descendant in 250 after four generations. The usual chances of poverty for the rest of the population are much, much higher than 7% – estimates in most developed countries vary from two to four times the prevalence. This is why transmitted deprivation has largely been abandoned as an explanatory model.

Sub-cultural explanations

The term 'culture' refers to the way in which a society adapts to its circumstances; Valentine describes a culture as an 'adaptive response' to 'environmental conditions and historical circumstances'.[243] A sub-culture is used, slightly more loosely, to refer to the way the way in which a sector of that society adapts. Poverty tends to imply, in many societies, a common experience of marginality and low status; and, in so far as poor people adapt their behaviour to their circumstances, there may well be a sub-culture of poverty.

Poor people are often described as a large, alien group. The idea of the 'underclass' is one in a long line of terms used for the poor: in the 19th century they were 'the abyss' or 'the submerged tenth', in the early 20th century they became 'degenerates', and in the post-war period they were 'problem families' or 'hard to reach'. Many of the terms, Matza comments wryly, convey the sense that poor people are a bit of a pain in the neck.[244]

During the War on Poverty in the US, the idea that took hold most strongly was the idea of the 'culture of poverty'. Oscar Lewis, an anthropologist, had carried out a study of a handful of poor Latin American families in Mexico and Puerto Rico. Lewis's studies, brilliantly and evocatively written in what seemed to be the voice of the family members, described a compelling picture of life in the slums. Lewis summarises some of the major characteristics as follows:

> On the family level, the major traits of the culture of poverty are the absence of childhood as a specially prolonged and protected stage in the life cycle, early initiation into sex, free unions or consensual marriages, a relatively high incidence of the abandonment of wives and children, a trend towards female- or mother-centred families ... a strong disposition to authoritarianism, lack of privacy, verbal emphasis on family solidarity which is only rarely achieved because of sibling rivalry, and competition for limited goods and maternal affection.
>
> On the level of the individual, the major characteristics are a strong feeling of marginality, of the helplessness, of dependence and of inferiority. ... Other traits include a high incidence of maternal deprivation, of orality, of weak ego structure, confusion of sexual

identification, a lack of impulse control, a strong present-time orientation with relatively little ability to defer gratification and to plan for the future, a sense of resignation and fatalism, a widespread belief in male superiority, and a high tolerance for psychological pathology of all sorts.[245]

This account has attracted a great deal of criticism. Valentine treats it as a gross generalisation based on one family: he calls it 'a middle-class rationale for blaming poverty on the poor'.[246] It is difficult to know whether this is justified. On one hand, Lewis's studies are careful, closely observed, and they paint a recognisable picture of the lives of many people. On the other, they also tend to be ambiguous, sensational and occasionally lurid. Looking at Lewis's detailed analysis – which comes, not in the main text of his books, but in his extended forewords – there is some confusion between poverty, character and culture. Relating to poverty, 'lack of privacy' is not a behavioural issue; it happens because people do not have an environment which allows them privacy. 'Competition for limited goods' happens because people do not have goods.

The other elements, however, are much less clearly identifiable with poverty. The issues of character – authoritarianism, feelings of marginality and inferiority, weak egos, fatalism and so forth – can certainly be found among poor people, but they can also be found among people who are not poor. Indeed, all of the personal characteristics that Lewis describes have been described in another classic psychological study, *The authoritarian personality*[247], which was criticised for a sample that was biased towards middle-class membership. Some people may well be like the family that Lewis describes; but it is not obvious that it has much to do with poverty.

This leaves a range of other factors to explain, including differences in sexual behaviour, domestic arrangements and family break-up. It is at least arguable that this is a cultural adaptation to poverty. Marital breakdown is clearly related to poverty and unemployment, and it looks very much as if it is a direct consequence.[248] The argument is controversial, but unemployed males are unable to act in the traditional role of the breadwinner; divorce is often in the woman's economic interests. That would explain the connection between poverty and mother-centred families. There is less marital breakdown when employment prospects improve.

Sullivan argues that the problem with past studies on the 'culture of poverty' is not that there is no culture, but that they have been more concerned with pathology than with adaptive responses.[249] It has to be true that poor people behave differently from better-off people. That is part of what poverty means. If poverty consists of the inability to participate in society, of living without the amenities and patterns of life that other people have, they *have* to behave differently. What is not true is that they choose to live that way. We know they do not choose it, because most poverty in developed economies is relatively short term. When people have the choice, they do not stay poor.

Resource-based explanations

Resource-based explanations for poverty are based on a simple argument: that people are poor because there are not enough resources to go round. Individual explanations might help to understand which people will become poor – it should not be surprising that low educational attainment, racial disadvantage or disability are linked with poverty – but we do not need to understand poverty in those terms, or terms of character, behaviour or culture. If there are not enough resources, some people will be poor whatever we do.

We have seen one example of this in the case of homelessness (Box 2 in Chapter Two): wherever there are not enough houses or land, someone is going to be left without a place to live. The same kind of argument can be made about economic resources in developing countries, and (more debatably) about food. When Thomas Malthus wrote about the evils of over-population, he was concerned that the exponential growth of the human population would lead inevitably to shortage.[250] Malthus's predictions were wrong, partly because he failed to understand the nature of technological progress, but also because he could not have anticipated the profound effect that economic development and the changing role of women would have on childbearing. The general pattern has been that as economies grow, the size of families falls. Part of the reason has been the fall in infant mortality – one of the main reasons people in poor countries want big families is to have some chance that a child will survive (see Box 13). No less important has been the delay in childbearing which follows the development of education and careers for women.

The idea that people will breed irresponsibly enjoys periodic resurgences in popularity, and certainly many of the critiques of the developing world begin from the supposition that the central problem is that they have too many people.[251] There is supposed to be a 'population explosion', which is going eventually to lead to some kind of disaster. *Limits to growth*, a phenomenally popular account of the 1970s, argued that population was growing to a potentially catastrophic level.[252] Malthus can be defended: he was writing two centuries ago, and long-term prediction is difficult. The new Malthusians[253] do not have the same excuse. If anything, the problem in developed economies is the opposite: there may not be enough people being born to sustain economic production and development.

Limits on resources are only true in the short term. Resources are not fixed; as economies grow and develop, there are more resources to share around. The capacity to grow depends on a range of resources, including (among others) water supplies, energy and land. The 'law of the minimum' implies that shortage in any essential factor will limit growth in the others.[254] There is no reason to believe, however, that any absolute limit is likely to be reached, ever. That is not how economics works. What happens, instead, is that as items become scarce, the relative costs change: alternatives which were initially more expensive become relatively less costly than current options are. One form of energy can be replaced by another, water can be obtained through desalination, and so on. The alternatives will usually be more expensive than current commodities, but they are possible, practical and available. Growth is not, then, subject to limits.

Box 13: Population and poverty

Population in the poorest parts of the world continues to grow; in developing countries, the trend has reversed. The trend in Table 13.1 is as plain as a pikestaff. People have more babies in places where their babies are more likely to die.

The main predictor of fertility is risk to life. The main predictor of risk to life is poverty. Since the 1960s there has been a striking improvement in life expectancy and infant mortality rates, even in poor countries. Greater survival tends to suggest an increasing population, unless it is counterbalanced by a reduction in fertility rates. Fertility rates have started to fall in the South American countries and the Middle East, but this has not been happening in the poorest countries (mainly African). If these countries are able to replicate the improvements in other poor parts of the world (and there is no intrinsic reason why they cannot), the birth rate in Africa will also fall.

Table 13.1: Basic demographic indicators[255]

	Life expectancy at birth	Crude birth rate		Fertility rate	Under-5s mortality rate		GNP per capita $, 2003
		1970	2003		1960	2003	
Sub-Saharan Africa	46	48	40	5.4	278	175	496
Middle East/ North Africa	67	45	27	3.4	249	56	1,465
South Asia	63	41	26	3.3	244	92	511
East Asia/ Pacific	69	35	16	2	208	40	1,426
Latin America	70	37	22	2.5	153	32	3,311
Former Eastern bloc	70	21	13	1.6	112	41	2,036
Industrialised countries	78	17	12	1.7	39	6	28,337

One of the obvious ways in which the trend can be encouraged is by taking measures to protect infant health – not simply through medical care, but by providing the infrastructure of water supplies, drainage and sanitation that are critical to public health. Another important approach has been to extend the rights of women, which has been a major factor in reducing childbirth. As things improve, population growth will fall. As a former Indian minister, Karan Singh, argued: 'The path to family planning in every country lies through the eradication of poverty, which in fact has historically been the main cause of over-population. ... The best contraceptive is development'.[256]

Structural explanations

A structural explanation is one that sees poverty as following from the structure of society – that is, from the organisation of social relations, such as class, status and power. Wherever society is unequal, some people will be richer and others will be poorer. Inequality limits the resources of people who are disadvantaged, and the problems of poverty follow as night follows day. 'Critical' analysts see disadvantage and exclusion as the product of systematic biases and divisions in the social structure. The key social divisions include the divisions of gender and 'race'; there are other systemic biases working against disabled people, older people and people with learning disabilities. At the core of 'critical' explanations is the argument that outcomes are not produced either randomly, or, as many economists would have it, through the complex interactions of individuals; they are conditioned by the social structure. People's chances, opportunities, and the circumstances of their lives are not fixed, but their prospects are limited, and it can be difficult to break away from the disadvantages that are built into the system. The game is rigged. Many texts on poverty in developed economies examine the experience of a range of disadvantaged groups, like women or disabled people. The reason for this kind of focus is not to show that such people are invariably poor, but to explain the kind of problems that need to be addressed. The central issue in most critical explanations is not poverty, but the inequality that perpetuates it.

The other kind of structural explanation sees poverty not as part of society, but as a product of it. Marxist explanations are an example: poverty is the by-product of a 'capitalist' system which rewards returns to capital and penalises economic redundancy. Functionalist explanations, which consider poverty and unemployment as necessary for society, are another example.[257] These explanations are facile. It does not follow that, because things happen, someone must have wanted it that way.

Agency explanations

The final class of explanations are those which see poverty as the result of the action or inaction of others. People are described as poor, for example, because of the failure of the welfare state – though that seems to imply that the welfare state has failed to make the difference it should. This sort of explanation tends to be incomplete, because formal institutions can only respond to poverty after poverty has occurred; there has to be some other explanation as well.

It is often argued that people are poor because of what such institutions do. In developing countries, poverty is often represented as the result of the actions of government or international organisations. Governments in the developing world may be thought to add to the problems, through inefficiency and corruption, at the same time as the actions of foreign governments and international organisations are seen as reinforcing the dependency and economic handicaps of the developing world. These points are developed further in Chapter Fourteen.

Equally, there are criticisms in developed economies of agency intervention. Some commentators see poverty as the product of misconceived government action, or 'government failure'.[258] This argument tends to reflect the position of the political right. Conservatives believe that provision for poor people has undesirable effects on the way that people behave, fostering dependency and reducing motivation. Free-market liberals argue that the provision of welfare has a distorting influence on the economy, producing the very conditions it is intended to avoid. These arguments are contentious, and not at all well supported by the evidence; the implication that poverty is aggravated where greater welfare provision is made is transparently false. (It is striking that they are made most vigorously in the US, a country with markedly inferior social provision to others.[259])

What is true, by contrast, is that government action may determine the ways in which poverty is understood and perceived. An example is the issue of retirement. Ageing may be natural, but there is nothing 'natural' about retirement; it is mainly an institution of the 20th century, introduced partly out of a sense that older people deserve support, partly out of a moral concern about their poverty, but also a practical way of regulating labour markets. Older people are increasingly expected and required to retire, and so to become dependent. The issue is referred to in Chapter Nine as 'structural dependency'. (The same idea applies to younger people in developed countries, who are spending more and more time in education.) We cannot clearly say whether people would not be poor without government action, and the question hardly makes sense; the way things are is the way they have been shaped. There is, then, an argument to say that the dependency of older people is indeed the result of government action, and that if they are poor, it consequently becomes the responsibility of government.

Explanations and moral judgements

In general, the moral condemnation of poverty tends to be associated with the first three views. Pathological views can be identified with poverty as the fault of the poor person, or the result of their actions. If it is their own fault, the argument runs, then it is not our responsibility to get them out of it. Genetic views tend to represent poverty as, in some way, the just and proper outcome for poor people. Sub-cultural arguments have been used to represent poor people as mad, bad and dangerous to know. It may not be their fault they are like that, but we do not want to touch them with a ten-foot pole. By contrast, structural views tend to be associated with the moral responsibility of society: if it is the fault of society, then it is up to society to sort it out. Similarly, views based on external agency suggest that government has a moral responsibility (even if, in some views, the moral responsibility of government is to stop doing what is causing the problem).

This is not very far away from the way the camps are lined up, but it is still oversimplified. The first problem is that the explanations for poverty are not genuinely exclusive. On one hand, individual and family-based explanations for poverty cannot be enough to explain why people are poorer or richer. There has to be some mechanism to translate this into social outcomes. Saying that people become poor because of laziness, incompetence or bad luck assumes a social structure in which these things are rewarded or punished. For that to happen, society has to be organised to make that possible. On the other hand, structural explanations identify the processes by which people become poor, but not which individuals it will happen to. In the competition for resources and status, those people who lose out are likely to include those who are less able, those who are disadvantaged, and those who have made bad decisions. If we want, then, we can take a structural view at the same time as we apply other explanations.

The second problem is that moral judgement does not necessarily follow from the kind of explanation we have for poverty. It may be true that society is organised as a competition between individuals, in which people are rewarded and punished for their actions. It is very debatable that what people get is determined by their own actions, but let us suppose for the moment that it is true. This leaves some relevant moral questions unresolved. One is whether the rewards and punishments are appropriate. We do not reward and punish people for all the consequences of their actions; for example, we do not punish people for smoking tobacco, which has devastating consequences for their own health and for public health, and we do not have rewards and punishments for the consequences of using motor cars. Why, then, should we think that rewards and punishments are appropriate to issues like unemployment and family responsibility? Another question is whether rewards and punishments are proportionate. A woman's decision to have a child can be much more devastating than the consequences, for example, of the decision of a criminal to burgle a house. If we really want to organise society to reward morally desirable behaviour and to punish undesirable behaviour, something is very wrong. And then there is a further, rather more fundamental question: is it really right, in principle, that rewards should go to the most successful – that 'to him who hath shall be given'?

The third problem is that the way things are is not necessarily the way they should be. Society is complex, and often irrational. Rewards, privilege and status are only loosely related to people's contributions to society, if at all. What happens does not have to make sense at all, let alone offer neatly ordered moral lessons for primary school children. If explanations for poverty work as a description of society, they are unlikely to point directly to specific moral conclusions. Conversely, if they do point to obvious moral conclusions, they are unlikely to be accurate descriptions.

FOURTEEN

Why poor countries stay poor

Although the kinds of explanation in the previous chapter can be fairly generally applied, they are implicitly focused on poverty in developed economies. The main issue they address is why some poor people are poor when others are not. The same arguments are found in developing countries – about whether poor people are to blame for their own condition, about resources, about social inequality and the structure of power. But it is difficult to understand poverty in developing countries within the same frame of reference. Poverty is global. Even by the very conservative standards of the World Bank, it affects nearly half the population of the world. We need to explain why the conditions of poverty in some parts of the world are so widespread, so general, and so persistent.

There are differences between the circumstances of different countries. The term 'developing countries' covers countries in a wide range of situations – various classifications are used by international organisations, including for example low-income countries (LICs), heavily indebted poor countries (HIPCs), and least developed countries (LDCs). Some economies are undergoing rapid development; some are in a process of transition. Some have only a marginal economic status, and some are not developing at all, but going backwards. Some countries are much poorer than others. The argument that a country can be poor depends, of course, on the same kind of argument as that made in Chapter Five – that poverty can apply to people collectively, not just individually. Some economists refer to the idea that one country is poorer than another by the odd-sounding term of 'poverty dominance'[260]; dominance measures are based on relative rankings. The point of using them is to show that, even if the terms on which measurements are made differ, one country might still emerge consistently as more disadvantaged than another.[261] Focusing on the poorest countries helps to identify the processes through which global poverty persists.

Internal problems

Some countries, it can be argued, are poor because there is something in their circumstances that prevents them from developing economically. The suggestion that poor countries are poor because of their own circumstances may seem to parallel views based on pathological views of poverty. It happens, as it does in pathological arguments, that there is a suggestion of moral disapproval in some commentaries. This is not necessary to the explanation, however. Several factors might have this kind of effect.

The failure to develop. One possible explanation for poverty is, simply enough, that nothing happens to stop it. The characteristic patterns of traditional society – particularly dependence on subsistence agriculture – are stable and long lasting. Few societies have not felt the influence of the changing world outside, but that is not enough to lead to development. There is nothing inevitable about growth. In *The stages of economic growth*, Rostow suggests that growth is a process which some countries go through while others do not.[262] For economic development to be possible, countries need a degree of development to have happened already. They need an infrastructure of communications, transport and education. They need the structure and practices of a working market – systems of exchange, of finance, banking and property law. (Developing these systems has become a major focus on intervention by international organisations.) For Rostow, successful growth depends on the national economy achieving a critical mass, or 'takeoff'. Rostow's argument might seem persuasive if we focus on the countries which have gone through rapid economic growth – the 'little tigers' of South East Asia, or the Chinese economy. But it works less well as a description of many economies in transition, like Turkey or India; middle-income countries which have made more gradual progress, like Uruguay or Mexico; or countries which seem to be declining economically, like Sierra Leone and the Democratic Republic of the Congo.[263] Because there are so many routes to development, it is difficult to see what route the least developed countries, like those in Sub-Saharan Africa, ought to follow.

Geographical limitations. A second view is that some countries have natural disadvantages. It cannot be coincidence, Todaro and Smith comment, that the world's developing countries are nearly all in tropical or sub-tropical climate zones.[264] This has immediate implications for water supply, agriculture and public health.

Vulnerability to natural disasters may affect economic development. Poorer countries, like richer countries, suffer a range of disasters, such as earthquakes, floods and eruptions. The same can be said of some richer countries, but the poorer countries may not have the resources or the capacity to recover afterwards. The impact of global warming offers a potential example – potential, because it is about what might happen, rather than what has happened. Climate change implies a change in economic and social change, and change tends to be disruptive. Where conditions are changing, the people who are most likely to be affected adversely are those whose circumstances are less adaptable. Those people are usually the poorest. *New Scientist* mentions five delta areas in particular, where millions of people are at risk: they are the Bengal delta in Bangladesh, the Mekong delta in Vietnam, the Yangtze in China, the Nile in Egypt and Godavari in India.[265] If sea levels rise, the Netherlands will be able to take the steps to protect its citizens; Bangladesh will not. Conversely, if Greenland becomes habitable, the people who will gain will be those who are able to move to Greenland, and they are probably not going to be the people who are displaced from Central Africa because of drought. Most of the strategies relating to global warming, like the Kyoto agreement, are concerned with preventing the perceived causes of climate change, not with protecting people from its effects. That may reduce risk, but it does not reduce vulnerability, and a marginal reduction in risk does little to compensate for the potentially devastating consequences of changing circumstances. From the perspective of helping the world's poor, most current policies on climate change are misconceived.

Natural resources clearly make a difference. Whereas some countries have abundant resources, such as oil, others have none. (It is possible, however, for a country to be rich in natural resources, and yet remain poor; the Congo is the most obvious example.) Thirty developing countries have no sea borders – examples are Nepal, Chad, Afghanistan and Bolivia. Many are inaccessible and remote in other ways. This is hardly an adequate explanation for poverty; the same problems might be said to apply to Switzerland. But these countries are dependent on their neighbours for infrastructure and access to world markets, and those neighbours also have limited development. They are also likely to be affected by the politics, administrative practices and the stability of neighbouring countries.[266] Geography does matter, but the political geography is at least as important as the physical geography.

Ill health. Ill health is a consequence of poverty, but it is also a cause of it. It causes poverty directly, by impairing people's ability to function, and indirectly, because conditions in which children die push people to have larger families. Because many diseases are communicable, the ill health of some people affects others. One of the concepts used in relation to public health is 'herd immunity'; there comes a point when, because most of the population is resistant to disease, others who are not resistant will not get it, because it is not likely to be passed on. The opposite is not quite true, but it comes close. If too many people in a population are vulnerable, and physical resistance is lowered by poor nutrition, the risks of diseases spreading are maximised. This presents problems for health care, with excessive demand and limited resources. An illustration of the cumulative effects is infant mortality. The problems of infant mortality are complex, but the primary immediate causes are respiratory ailments and diarrhoeal disease and problems relating to the birth process. Taken together, these account for about three quarters of all infant mortality.[267] The combination of vulnerability, communicable disease and limited health care can be devastating. Box 14 reviews some of the key health problems.

Box 14: Ill health

Many of the recent concerns about ill health have focused on the AIDS pandemic in Southern Africa. But AIDS is only one of many disorders that are so widespread that they constitute an obstacle to development. The WHO has calculated Disability Adjusted Life Years attributable to diseases: Table 14.1 is based on its figures.[268]

Table 14.1: Disability Adjusted Life Years (DALYs) lost through ill health

	DALYs lost – World	% of all DALYs lost	% of DALYS lost – Africa
Infectious and parasitic diseases	350,333	23.5	51.9
including			
• TB	34,736	2.3	2.6
• HIV/AIDS	84,458	5.7	17.7
Diarrhoeal disease	61,966	4.2	6.4
Malaria	46,486	3.1	11.3
Respiratory infections	94,604	6.3	9.8
Nutritional deficiencies	34,417	2.3	2.6
Malignant neoplasms (cancers)	75,545	5.1	0.8
Sense organ disorders	69,381	4.7	2.5
Cardiovascular diseases	148,190	9.9	3.0
Respiratory diseases	55,153	3.7	1.5
Injuries	181,991	12.2	8.5
including			
• road traffic accidents	38,676	2.6	2.0
• violence	21,429	1.4	1.5
• war	6,328	0.4	0.9

The figures are not reliable – they are rough estimates – and there has to be the suspicion that some of the ailments in the developed world may be better recorded than equivalent problems in developing countries. The table gives some useful pointers to problems. The problems of developed economies are often associated with ageing, which is why cardiovascular diseases, cancers and sensory disorders are less prominent in Africa. The problems of Africa are much more likely to be associated with infective and parasitic disorders: AIDS and malaria are particularly prominent, and they account for just over half the recorded problems in those categories. That still leaves many more to account for. The WHO has expressed concern that too much emphasis on communicable diseases in anti-poverty strategies leaves major gaps in health improvement strategies – such as dealing with the damage caused by smoking.[269] A comprehensive strategy for health has to go much wider.

Human development. Societies where human development is limited are also likely to suffer limited economic development. Human development is closely linked with economic development, but it is not directly equivalent. Some economic activity, in the context of developing countries, has little direct connection with the activity of the population: for example, in some countries, oil production benefits only an elite, while in others, Todaro suggests, trade is often between richer countries and foreign residents.[270] Some countries with relatively limited GDPs have achieved levels of life expectancy and education that are disproportionate to their income: examples are Cuba, Madagascar, Ecuador and some of the republics of the former Soviet Union. Others, with much more favourable economic resources, have relatively low human development: examples are the oil-rich countries of Iran and Saudi Arabia.[271]

There are clearly strong links between economic and human development. The richest countries are also those with the most generous social provisions. But it does not follow that economic development is required before social provision is possible. Mohammed ul Haq suggests: 'We were taught to take care of our GNP as this will take care of poverty. Let us reverse this and take care of poverty as this will take care of the GNP'.[272] The argument rests on three main propositions. The first is that where resources are more evenly spread, it creates a greater spur to economic activity than when they are concentrated. Second, poverty lowers economic productivity, and action to relieve poverty consequently increases it. Third, participation in society acts as an incentive for greater economic activity.[273]

Governance. Government affects people's lives in many ways. The central problem is to create a structure which makes economic and social development possible. The system of law is basic: the establishment of a system of property rights is one of the crucial elements in being able to participate in a formal economy; an example referred to in the course of this book has been the problem of women's rights. (Dollar and Kraay claim a direct statistical association between the structure of property rights and economic development.[274] This may be, as the authors claim, because property rights are a fundamental precondition of development, but might also be that the development of a formal economy is marked by the development of property rights.)

Equally, there have to be the mechanisms and institutions to make governance possible. The governments of developing countries, whatever their intentions, often have limited capacity to implement decisions. The Poverty Reduction Strategy Papers (PRSPs) prepared for the World Bank and the International Monetary Fund put a considerable emphasis on the development of such structures.[275] PRSPs may seem strange documents, because on the face of the matter they seem to contain a lot of material that is not directly concerned with poverty reduction. The central focus of many falls on governance. Sometimes the focus falls on structures of government and law, but 'governance' is much wider than either. Often the structure through which economic and political development can be governed depends on a partnership of government, voluntary, commercial and international organisations. The PRSPs have actively promoted participation, partnership and the development of economic, legal and political systems.

The world's poorest countries are often badly governed. In part, this reflects a limited capacity – where government has limited powers, it is often more difficult to protect the vulnerable. Bad government is not, however, just a matter of what is not done. One of the features that comes strongly out of research on poverty is the extent to which government is part of the problem, rather than the solution. Some governments act deliberately to make people's lives worse. In some cases, government represents dominant racial or tribal factions. Many governments are despotic, and would sooner respond to dissent by removing the dissidents than by responding to the criticism. Police and government institutions often harass people who are poor. Chapter Ten pointed to the importance of democratic procedures, and the rule of law. Although these issues can sometimes seem tangential to the issues of poverty, they are intimately connected.

Economic management. It is not possible to review every approach to economic management, but some models have been particularly influential in developing countries. In the 1950s and 1960s the two dominant models were Keynesian and *dirigiste*. The dominant models nowadays are liberal and corporatist.

- The *Keynesian* model was based on a managed, mixed economy. Keynesianism used fiscal controls, such as tax and interest rates, and public spending, to regulate the overall production in an economy. Keynesianism played a major part in the regeneration of Europe and America after the depression, by using public spending to regenerate depressed economies. Its application in Brazil in the early late 1950s, in a much less developed economy, generated a demand that the economy was unable to satisfy; it led to massive inflation, a major financial crisis and military takeover.
- *Dirigisme* refers to a government-run economy. The idea was promoted, in different ways, through Stalinism, Maoism and a range of approaches in Africa and Southern Asia, such as the attempts of Julius Nyerere in Tanzania to promote a combination of collectivist socialism along with traditional African solidarity. The essential elements were central state control, the direction of production and labour by government command, and a push for rapid development. The deficiencies of this approach are taken for granted nowadays. Its appeal to developing countries should not be underestimated, however; it seemed to offer a radical means to mobilise resources to create industrial production.
- The *liberal* model has argued for free markets, the free movement of capital, engagement in global trade and the development of production and infrastructure through the private market. Neo-classical economists argued that the core problem of the least developed economies had been the restrictions imposed by national governments.[276] In the 1980s, the

International Monetary Fund and the World Bank promoted 'structural adjustment', a particular model of economic reform for developing countries – creating opportunities for international business, imposing strict financial discipline, increasing inequality and cutting the public sector. Even when this worked, it generally increased the vulnerability of the poor.[277] When it did not, it could have very detrimental effects, because it weakened investment in human capital and cut away the main social protections that poorer people might have had.[278]

- The *corporatist* model depends on cooperation and coordination between a range of partners; the role of the state is to engage, plan and negotiate. This model is favoured in many of the PRSPs. While still reflecting an emphasis of private commercial activity, it also reflects the desire to develop government through partnership and to build a capacity for corporate strategic planning.

The management, and mismanagement, of national economies is heavily emphasised in many commentaries on the progress of individual countries.[279] This emphasis is understandable, partly because the issues relate to the factors which governments can control, and partly because the world is full of economists with knives and forks who are looking for something to cut. It is easy, however, to exaggerate the scope for action. Typically the tools available to manage an economy include fiscal policy, taxation, monetary policy, exchange controls and trade. Whatever governments in developing countries might like to do, they do not necessarily have the structures in place to do it.[280] Taxing people's personal income, for example, depends on an extensive system of reporting and monitoring, generally with the cooperation of employers; taxing expenditure depends on the integration of commerce into the formal economy; and controlling the money supply depends on cooperation with the banking system. ('Money' is what people are willing to accept; some transitional economies have multiple, competing currencies.) There is sometimes a naive assumption that models which are used in developed western economies should be applied in developing countries. An example is the literature on 'targeting'. There are many possible ways of identifying target groups, and most of them have been tried in developing countries.[281] Measures which depend on sophisticated individual assessment, like means testing, are often hopelessly impractical. It can be difficult to monitor the financial status of a household, where, for example, people living in settlements are not just not part of the formal economy, but have no postal address. The emphasis on development in practice tends to depend not so much on central planning and control as on incremental improvements in economic activity, based on a process of regulation, negotiation and compromise.

Corruption. The problem of corruption goes beyond government. It manifests itself typically in problems of developing infrastructure, when constructors cannot be relied on to use the materials which are being paid for; in administration, where costs and timescales become unpredictable; and in the development of services, because in a society where no one can be trusted to manage a fund, it is difficult to establish systems of mutual support needed for social protection or health care. Savedoff and Huffman argue that corruption is likely to occur when opportunities exist. The transparency of procedures, the existence of alternatives for consumers and the institutional structures all play a part in fostering or limiting the scope for corruption.[282]

Corruption is not confined to developing countries, but one has to ask why it is so prevalent in those countries.[283] The first, obvious problem is about relative income. If it is difficult to bribe officials in the West, it may simply be because few bribes are large enough to tempt someone who stands to lose a secure monthly salary and a pension. A second problem is the underdevelopment of market procedures: sometimes people demand illegal payments for things (like providing medical treatment when it is supposed to be free) which in other societies they would be able to charge for legitimately. A third issue concerns systems of financial monitoring. It goes without saying that information management is better developed in more developed economic systems, but this is not why procedures against fraud are more effective in those countries. Many of the procedures used in developed countries to protect against fraud were built up in the course of the 19th and early 20th centuries. Examples include accounting practice, the division of financial authority and audit. In most public services in developed countries, financial decisions are not made by individuals, but are cross-checked by a series of people at different stages of the process. The new information technology has unstitched part of these procedures, and some of the traditional methods of monitoring have been replaced, but the principles still hold good. Fourth, and not least, there is the role of the institutions which are engaged in corrupt practice – including multinational corporations and independent private companies from the developed world.[284] The lack of enforcement, monitoring and penalties for firms involved in corrupt practice gives little reason for it to stop.

Armed conflict. Although there have been times when military expenditure has been associated with expanding public services[285], the general growth in military expenditure since the 1970s has had a detrimental effect on economic growth and human development.[286] Beyond that, many poor countries have inter-ethnic conflict, insurrections or territorial disputes. Although war seems, by comparison with disease, to have a much more limited effect on death and disability (see Box 14), it has widespread ill effects. Armed conflict disrupts communications, displaces populations, prevents trade and obstructs development. Famines may occur, for example – as in Eritrea or Sudan – because armed conflict has prevented the movement of goods. Equally, poverty makes countries vulnerable to armed conflict; there is an association between low development and the risk of civil war.[287]

Relationships with other countries

International trade. In theory, all countries gain from specialisation and exchange. Wherever countries have a different potential to produce goods, they should be able to maximise output by specialising in the goods where they have a comparative advantage, and exchanging the production. This has been widely accepted as an argument for free trade. Protecting national industries, which might suffer in open competition, is generally frowned on. There are other arguments for protection – for example, preserving a capacity in areas which are essential to national defence, or protecting infant industries which otherwise will not be able to establish themselves in an uneven competition – but even these are strongly resisted.

In practice, however, the rules are rigged. Developing countries are not allowed access to markets in developed economies, or are allowed access only on unequal terms.[288] The UNDP comments that

> the world's highest trade barriers are erected against some of its poorest countries: on average the trade barriers faced by developing countries exporting to rich countries are three to four times higher than those faced by rich countries when they trade with each other.[289]

Infant industries in developing countries are suppressed by a range of restrictive practices, such as 'dumping', where firms charge high prices in their own domestic market but sell cheaply abroad. The EU restricts the importation of agricultural produce, primarily to protect its own farmers at the expense of its consumers. The US subsidises and protects a wide range of products. The most successful transitional economies have not relied on free trade; they have used a judicious mixture of protection, managed exchange rates and export promotion to overcome the barriers.[290]

Migration. Developing countries export labour to developed economies. Often this means that the most skilled and educated people work outside the country. 'Remittances', or the money they send home, are a major source of income to the countries. This poses a dilemma. On one hand, access to developed economies is a way of educating workers, gaining income and developing opportunities – though most of that depends on migrant workers eventually returning. On the other, the exportation of labour, expertise and entrepreneurs, a process which parallels the formation of richer and poorer areas at local level, almost certainly handicaps some aspects of domestic development.

Debt. Many of the poorest countries are heavily indebted. A joint paper from non-governmental organisations makes the telling point that 'the poorest countries in the world routinely spend more on debt repayments than they do on health'.[291] The sources of the debt are complex, and not simply related to government borrowing; the core of the problem rests in the net inflow or outflow of foreign exchange. Todaro and Smith identify a series of contributory factors: they include

- the effects on national income of reduced economic activity or reducing commodity prices;
- deficits in the balance of payments;
- capital outflows when residents move money abroad; and
- the cost of servicing the debt itself.[292]

The issue of debt has tended to dominate debates about relationships with developing countries. This is partly a moral judgement. Countries may feel they have no responsibility for the citizens of other countries, and they do not necessarily accept an argument that says that they should compensate for historic injustices. The issue of debt, by contrast, is immediate, both in terms of timing and in terms of current responsibility. Another reason is the nature of the debts. The foundation of some parts of the debts is questionable; some countries are being held accountable for lending to illegitimate, despotic regimes that have subsequently been displaced. The debate has also been driven by a strategic view, that arguments about the issue of debt are winnable in a way that debates about the relief of poverty are not. Poverty is a vast, intractable series of problems. The issue of debt is closely defined, and the emphasis on the injustice of debt has been persuasive to many governments; relief has now been granted to a limited number of the most heavily indebted poor countries. Gordon Brown, the UK Chancellor of the Exchequer, has stated:

> I see debt relief as both an economic and moral issue – an economic issue, because a mountain of inherited and hitherto immovable debt stands in the way of economic development in Africa and elsewhere and their full inclusion in world society. A moral issue, because unsustainable debt is a burden imposed from the past on the present, which is depriving millions of their chance of a future, preventing them breaking out of the vicious cycle of poverty, illiteracy and disease, preventing the investment in what is really necessary – the healing of the sick, the teaching of the children, and the advancement of economic opportunity for those denied it.[293]

Agency explanations. In the same way as the internal problems of countries parallel pathological views about poverty, the external factors which lead countries to remain poor can be seen in terms of agency and structural explanations, sometimes referred to as 'poverty production'.[294] The actions of other countries have shaped the conditions of poor countries through colonialism, cultural dominance, armed conflict and economic influence. Colonialism is an archetypal example; the colonial powers mainly acquired their colonies through physical force, and used the assets, including labour and natural resources, for their own purposes. Many critics of western policy in the developing world see it in terms of 'neo-colonialism', the maintenance of quasi-colonial relationships through economic and political means.

Currently, much of the influence of developed countries on the least developed countries is expressed through three routes. One is the private sector, in the form of transnational companies. Transnational companies, and their national subsidiary companies, exercise their influence largely because of the economic benefits they bring – as employers, as purchasers and as the route to engaging people in the formal economy. Investment by foreign companies is welcome, because it introduces capital, enables the exploitation of resources, and generates revenue. At the same time, it can lead to a withdrawal of resources, reduce foreign exchange earnings, and, because of the kinds of arrangement which tend to be made, it can act to stifle local competition and markets. Transnational companies have also been criticised for exploitative conditions – including conditions like child labour that would not be acceptable in their home countries – and engagement in corruption; the alternative would not be for such companies to withdraw, but for them to clean up their act.

The second route is through international aid. Aid tends to be restricted, and it is often linked to economic activity. About a third is 'tied', which means that it is conditional on expenditure in the donating country. Third, there is the role of the international organisations, which are the principal mechanisms through which governments exert their influence. As a condition of financial support, including debt relief, the International Monetary Fund and the World Bank are increasingly using 'conditionality' – terms which countries have to comply with. For example, eligibility for the relief to HIPCs has depended on submission of PRSPs. The role of international organisations is deeply ambiguous. At one and the same time, organisations like the International Monetary Fund can be seen as beneficial structures, designed to help countries in difficulty, and as a means of imposing the will of dominant countries (and particularly of the US) on others. The UN has been designed simultaneously both to promote universal standards, and to prevent the intervention of countries in each others' affairs. International organisations do not speak with a single voice; they represent a range of factions, and different influences are dominant at different times.

Structural factors. The idea of 'structural dependency' has been used to explain the continuing disadvantage of developing countries. Some countries are locked into dependent relationships with richer countries, which on one hand facilitate basic patterns of economic development, but on the other take out the benefits, like labour and natural resources. Much of Latin America can be seen as structurally dependent on the US. André Gunder Frank argues that the pattern of dominance and dependency is replicated within regions and industrial sectors.[295] Lal argues, against this interpretation, that attempts to break away from relationships of dependency have been disastrous. If governments think that a relationship is exploitative, and limit or break off trade, it loses the benefits of economic development and of trade.[296] The attempt to develop independently is dangerously misconceived – the worst case is probably Kampuchea, where the determination to break away from world capitalism led to some of the greatest horrors of the 20th century.[297]

Even if the relationship between nations is not described in terms of 'dependency', there is still a case to think of the relationship as 'structural'. The relationship of Mexico to the US, or of North Africa to Europe, is conditioned by geographical proximity, history, culture and lines of communication. Patterns of trade and the development of economic specialisation are conditioned by that kind of link.

Developing policy

One of the clichés of work with poverty is the idea that to deal with it, we have to address the causes. This is a fallacy. The way into a problem is not the way out of it. If you fall into deep water, your understanding of gravity and fluid mechanics is not going to help very much; what matters is whether you know how to swim. The issues that matter here for the reduction of poverty are not the analyses of causal processes; they are the issues which help to identify issues and assess the character of the problems. It is important to know that a lack of infrastructure, the limited capacity of government and problems in getting access to markets are impeding development. It is not particularly helpful, for practical purposes, to know that the situation relates to a history of colonial exploitation, structural dependency or economic mismanagement. In Part Seven, I plan to move on to the kinds of response which are available to deal with the problems.

Part Seven
Responses to poverty

FIFTEEN

Responding to poverty

Responses to poverty

There are many ways of responding to poverty. Parts One to Five of this book were based on an examination of eleven main categories of definition. They can be applied in a range of fields or spheres of activity, like nutrition, housing, employment, health care and so on. It is not possible to review every combination. What this Part tries to do, instead, is to make some generalisations about the way in which governments and societies respond to poverty.

Poor relief. The most basic response has been to attempt to relieve poverty. If people are in need, they can be given the things they need – food, clothing, shelter and so forth. If they are in a weak economic position, short of resources, or disadvantaged, they can be given money or resources. This was the model of poor relief in mediaeval Europe, and it has carried on in a similar form ever since.

Poor relief gets a terrible press, and a few things ought to be said in its favour. Poor relief is often what poor people need. There is a slogan used by some charities: 'give a man a fish, and you feed him for a day. Teach him to fish and you feed him for life'. This is staggering arrogance. We have tools that people in subsistence cultures do not have, and we can use those to increase productivity. But why do we imagine that people in developing countries do not have the basic skills for survival? Could we survive under the same constraints? Do international organisations really know more about fishing than people who spend their lives doing it? There are more immediate issues to deal with. People who are starving, landless, or the victims of civil war cannot plough land, fish or produce clothing for European supermarkets. Wherever people have problems, there is a case for trying to deal with those problems directly. Poor relief may be all that is needed. In developed countries in particular, poverty is often temporary; people need relief to tide them over. And without poor relief, we might add, the options for doing many of the other things that people want to do with poor people, like social education or preventive work, are very limited.

Many debates about responding to poverty are concerned with the most effective way of distributing poor relief. Debates about 'targeting', in particular, are mainly concerned with how relief should go to poor people – typically, whether there should be some form of selection, and what the basis of the selection should be. It is possible, for example, to focus on the people who are most likely to escape poverty; those who are most in need; and on groups or areas in poverty.[298]

Equally, poor relief can involve distribution in cash, or in kind. Cash assumes a market economy, and the ability to buy things; injecting cash into a famine does not necessarily make things better. Distribution in kind, conversely, can have its own problems. Sometimes the things which are distributed are done badly, like aircraft drops of food (because they can be monopolised by the people who are strongest); sometimes they are the wrong things, like the distribution of dried cow's milk to African countries. In many cases, however, distribution in kind is an essential first step. The provision of shelter, food or medical care can help to establish a basis for other forms of provision. It may not be as good as an individually tailored programme to respond to the needs of each individual, but it needs no apology.

Social protection. Social protection works principally by providing for predictable contingencies, like old age, sickness, disability and unemployment. People in these circumstances are not necessarily poor, but they may be likely to be poor if no provision is available.

Often, social protection is offered through insurance, but it can also be done through the general provision of social services (like the national health provision in some European countries). In many countries social protection has developed through the actions of government, but this is not true everywhere. Several countries developed social protection through the growth of mutual insurance, developed through a combination of occupational provision, voluntary societies or the action of trades unions. Where these schemes have become compulsory, the main effect has been to extend the provision down the social scale – compelling employers to make the same kind of provision for people on low incomes that other employees had made for them as part of their contracts of employment.

Social protection is not targeted on the poor, then, and it is debatable whether a focus on poverty is even a primary consideration. It is perhaps surprising, then, to discover that some of the national welfare systems which are most effective in dealing with poverty, like those in Northern Europe, have been based on the principle of social protection rather than poor relief.[299] The schemes which do best, like provision for older people in Sweden[300], are the ones which provide for people regardless of need.[301] Schemes which offer a 'safety net' do not do so well in securing a minimum income. If a system is based on support for everyone, poor people will also be helped. If it supports only the poor, some are likely to be excluded.

Strategic intervention. A common form of intervention has been the selection of a specific approach or set of measures, intended to respond to the characteristics of poverty that governments or social organisations believe are central. During the history of the Poor Law, when poverty was believed to be the result of idleness, provision was made to 'set the poor on work'. When it was seen as the result of sickness, provision was made for public health. When later it was reinterpreted as a problem of old age, policies to deal with poverty were policies for older people. This list could be endless. Although some policies and themes recur frequently, few aspects of poverty have not, at one time or another, become a central focus for action.

The link between these disparate approaches is a confidence that it is possible, not just to 'kill two birds with one stone', but to bring down the flock. It depends on the general view that problems are interconnected. Sometimes they are tied to a common cause. At the beginning of the 20th century, 'degeneracy' was seen as the root of 'mental deficiency', crime, poverty and social disorder.[302] Initially provision was made to isolate degenerates from the community; subsequently this stretched to sterilisation and eventually to extermination.[303] Sometimes attention is focused on a particular set of measures, like education or getting poor people to work, because this is seen as the answer to most problems. Complex problems are not treated in a complex way: decision makers try, instead, to find The Key, the simple solution that will unlock every other problem. We know enough about poverty by now to know that there is no key. There are many problems, and we need many responses. That does not mean that people are going to stop looking for one.

Prevention. Preventive action works by stopping people becoming poor in the first place. This is usually attempted by trying to deal with the causes of poverty. If poverty is caused by genetic inferiority, purge the lower breeds. If poverty results from lacking an economic market, introduce a free market. If poverty is caused by capitalism, bring down capitalism. But it seems abundantly clear that this kind of approach does not generally work. Part of the problem – certainly the problem in these three examples – is that the analysis of causes is often misconceived. Many of the worst, most destructive policies, have been fuelled by the conviction that the policy makers knew what the causes of the problem were. But this is not all of the problem. Part is that the responses which are chosen do not necessarily deal with the cause – like the misplaced attempts to respond to impoverished motherhood with sex education and even, heaven help us, pledges about chastity. Part is that there is no single cause.

Prevention works best in two circumstances. The first, which is relatively rare, is when the cause is correctly identified and the response is precise. An example is the unemployment of the 1930s, correctly identified at the time as the result of deficient demand, and dealt with (at least in some countries) through public works. The second is common, but gloriously imprecise: it happens where the improvement in living standards is so general that it deals with a range of problems along the way. This has been, more or less, the effect of economic development, of the type currently being experienced in China and South East Asia. It is not the answer to every problem, and it will not prevent poverty in all its forms, but it helps to turn an overwhelming set of problems into a merely enormous set.

Indirect responses. The final category of response is an odd one to include, but it is so widely and extensively used that it would leave a hole if it was not mentioned. With the best intentions, political responses to poverty are often hidden behind smoke and mirrors. Poverty is a serious moral issue, but it also attracts serious condemnation. In many countries, poverty is not dealt with directly at all. What happens instead is that some other issue comes to stand in for poverty. People who support the poor can console themselves that they are getting some way towards making a response; those who do not can continue to condemn the poor without a charge of inconsistency. In France, for many years, family benefits had this role. Family benefits were introduced in the 1930s, following an unlikely campaign of support combining the interests of feminist and Catholic organisations.[304] In a country where 'poverty' had never been part of the political dialogue – the discourse of exclusion, dating from the 1970s, is the nearest that French politics has come – generous support for families, including large families, young children and single parents, played a major role in offering practical support to a substantial proportion of the population.

It is difficult to say clearly how widespread this kind of approach really is, because the terms in which poverty are discussed are so muddled. Support for families, older people and unemployed workers clearly falls into this category. Arguably, urban regeneration, public housing and many educational policies can be seen in the same light. Part of the Millennium Development Goals (see Box 15) are based, rightly, on the immediate, direct relief of the problems of poverty. But others, including gender equality, primary education and environmental sustainability, are also concerned with policies that are acceptable and desirable in their own right, and likely to benefit the poor, without being targeted clearly and directly at them.

Conversely, policies which appear to be about poverty may not be. In the US, material that is ostensibly about poverty – like the War on Poverty of the 1960s – is sometimes used as cover for an even more charged and sensitive issue, which is the debate on 'race'. Foreign aid is often a means of promoting domestic industrial interests, rather than helping economic development in poorer countries. The International Monetary Fund's work on poverty – particularly the PRSPs – has as much to do with governance and political stability as it does with poor people. We need to shimmy away from the idea that policies are selected with a particular purpose in mind, and that they are adapted for that purpose. Policies are negotiated by people with a range of interests, and refracted through a series of distorting lenses.

Box 15: The Millennium Development Goals

The Millennium Development Goals have been adopted by the 191 members of the UN. They commit the UN, by 2015, to:
* eradicate extreme poverty and hunger *(actually, to reduce the proportions by half)*
* achieve universal primary education
* promote gender equality and empower women
* reduce child mortality
* improve maternal health
* combat HIV/AIDS, malaria and other diseases
* ensure environmental sustainability and
* develop a global partnership for development.[305]

The Sachs report claims that 'the Millennium Development Goals are the most broadly supported, comprehensive, and specific poverty reduction targets the world has ever established.'[306]

In policy terms, the MDGs represent a shift from making policy by process or inputs – for example, giving a percentage of income in aid – to setting targets to achieve outcomes. The strategy identifies 18 targets, assessed by 48 tests.[307] For example, the aim of 'developing a global partnership for development' is intended to include:
* promoting a trading and financial system
* focusing on the special needs of the LDCs (including debt relief, and favourable terms of trade)
* addressing the needs of landlocked states and small islands
* dealing with debt
* developing work of young people
* arranging access to essential medication, and
* exploiting the benefits of new technologies.

Strategic approaches

Policy tends to develop piecemeal, and it emerges over a long period of negotiation, experimentation, adjustment and use. Policy analysts also use, though, a 'rational' model, which helps to identify the key stages in policy decisions. Policies begin with a statement of *aims* – what the policy is trying to achieve. They select from a range of alternative *methods*. They have to be *implemented*, or put into practice. And they are judged in terms of their *outcomes*. Any policy can be assessed in these terms.

Aims Policies for poverty have many different aims. In many cases they are meant to alleviate poverty, but equally they may be intended to contain it, to reduce it, or even to eliminate it. Because poverty has many different forms and aspects, there is no simple formula that can be used. There are two core problems. The first is that anti-poverty policies which work for one kind of poverty do not necessarily help with others. A policy which is designed to meet needs or to promote rights (reducing poverty in one sense) may increase dependency (exacerbating it in another). A policy which promotes employment and economic development may reinforce the disadvantage of those who cannot participate in the economic market. Promoting economic growth is sometimes done at the expense of inequality. None of these consequences is inevitable, but it does imply that partial responses may be unsatisfactory, and even, in some cases, self-defeating.

The second problem is that many aims are implicit, concealed, or guided by other principles. Suggestions for dealing with poverty are bedevilled by other concerns about life, the universe and everything. What will the effect be on the economy, on education, on culture, on family life, on religion, on personal relationships? The range of topics raised seems to have no limits. Many of the things written about in this book are subject to the same kinds of criticism, and it is not possible to deal with all of them. The best response, in the short term, is to address at least the most common objections – that responding to poverty tends to reduce economic performance (see Box 16), that it alters the character of the poor (debatable) and that it alters social relationships (which has to be true, though that is not necessarily an objection).

Methods. The main approaches to poverty were considered in the previous section, and they point to a wide range of possible alternatives for any interpretation of 'poverty'. In many political debates, discussions of methods tend to be trapped by the pattern of measures taken in the past. Practical men, Keynes once wrote, are often the slaves of some defunct economist. Responding to poverty involves much more than 'setting the poor on work' (the formula of the 1601 Poor Law), unemployment relief or income maintenance, but repeatedly political discussion of the issues locks into orbit around the same narrow range of options. Often the inheritance of the past dictates the fine detail of specific policies – like the constant harping in the UK about people being 'better off on the dole', a concept still interpreted in terms of the Victorian Poor Law, or the use of 'workfare' in some US states as a quasi-penal deterrent to dependency.

Implementation. The study of implementation helps to explain some of the discrepancies between the theory of how a policy ought to work and what actually happens on the ground. At the same time, some anti-poverty policies are currently focused almost exclusively on the process of implementation. PRSPs put a considerable weight on engagement of a range of actors: on partnership, consultation, and political negotiation. They put much less weight on achieving results. There are good arguments for this approach. Deficiencies in the process of government are central to many of the problems of developing countries. Often they lack the capacity to plan, to regulate, and to enforce political decisions. At the same time, it seems difficult to sustain the argument that improving governance is a precondition for poverty reduction. Neither economic development nor social protection has to depend on government intervention. Several countries have achieved major advances without the institutions of democracy – China is an obvious example. This implies that the emphasis on governance in PRSPs is motivated, not so much by the desire to deal with poverty, as with other issues, like political and economic liberalisation. Reforms in governance may be desirable, but they are neither necessary nor sufficient for poverty reduction.

Outcomes. The identification of outcomes takes us back, in a neat circle, to one of the issues we began with: how poverty can be identified and researched. The issue is not necessarily to measure effects accurately or precisely, but rather to get a clear indication of what the effects are. 'Targets', or performance indicators, can have a distorting effect on priorities: improvements in one issue, like the numbers of people in work or levels of income, often ignore effects in other ways, like problems of inequality or housing supply. The best approach, then, is to use a range of possible indicators, getting the fullest information for appraisal.

SIXTEEN

Policies for poverty

There is no obvious 'answer' to poverty. Because the problems are so diverse, it is never possible to deal with every issue. This book is concerned with general issues, though, and it should still be helpful to think generally about what can be done. This final chapter considers some of the main practical options for dealing with poverty.

What works?

For the most part, the question of what works, and what does not, depends on the context where it is applied. Many of the measures which have been used to help poor people have to be interpreted according to circumstances. The institution of public works, in the 'New Deal' of the 1930s, did much to get the US out of the depression; the same idea, applied in Brazil in the 1950s and early 1960s, led to economic collapse. Nevertheless, we can say with reasonable confidence that some things tend to work, and some don't.

An example might be individualistic measures, which aim to give poor people a better chance in competition with others. Measures of this sort don't work. They don't work, in general, because logically speaking they can't. In a game of 'musical chairs', children run around until the music stops, there are not enough chairs to sit on, and the person who is left standing is out. If one child runs faster, another will be left out instead. Even if everyone runs faster, someone will still be 'out'; it is built into the game. In the same way, in any system that relies on people competing more effectively, there will still be people who are left out. Giving people incentives, or getting them to try harder, might improve their individual prospects, but it is inherent in the nature of such measures that they cannot prevent poverty. That does not mean that special programmes like education and work training are pointless. They increase people's potential, and they can help to revitalise local economies. They could help reduce poverty, for example, fostering economic development because someone is able to use their new skills to start up a new enterprise. In other words, they work in so far as they have a collective impact – but not in so far as the focus is on the relative position of individuals.

Another policy that doesn't work, or at least that doesn't work adequately, is the attempt to deal selectively with some groups of poor people while excluding others. It is not uncommon for systems of social protection to make a distinction between unemployed people, disabled people and sick people. Some systems provide for some, and not for others. The problem with this approach is that when there is no provision, people in desperate straits have to deal with the system anyway, and the pressure becomes unsustainable. If, for example, provision is made for disability but not for sickness – a fairly common situation in the transitional economies of Eastern Europe – people with long-term illnesses have to present themselves as disabled, or they will not get support. If there is no provision for unemployed people, which happens in some US states, unemployed people have to apply as disabled or sick. In the days of the Poor Law, the provision made in the workhouse initially failed to make adequate provision for sickness and disability, and the provision for the non–disabled poor was inundated with people who were not fit for work. (This is why hospitals and public health were developed under the aegis of the Poor Law.)

If we ask, by contrast, what does work, three approaches to poverty seem to have had more success than others. They can all be justified as a direct response to the problems of poverty – or at least, to some understandings of those problems. They might also be seen as responding to the causes, but that depends on interpretation. But none of them has developed, historically, as a result of an understanding of the causes. They have gradually taken hold because, by comparison with the alternatives, they seemed to work.

The first is economic development, because it improves the standards which apply in a society overall. In the 1980s, it was often suggested that 'a rising tide lifts all boats', and that the benefits of growth would 'trickle down' to the poor. Both of those propositions are suspect. Mishra comments: 'a rising economic tide not only does not lift all boats, it can upturn, destroy and sink many boats'.[308] The casualties of economic development include people whose work is displaced in a changing economy, people who lose their role, people who do badly in competition. Increases in inequality are problematic, not just because inequality is corrosive socially, but because inequality can lead to rising prices as the competition for scarce resources increases. People whose resources are fixed, or whose resources do not grow at the same speed as others, lose out in that competition. There have been cases where economic development has been accompanied by falls in the living standards of the poorest.[309] Economic development is not a guarantee of human development.

Economic development is a good thing, though, in several other ways. First, many people will benefit. Economic development provides people with increased standards of living and material goods. The effect of increasing resources is not that resources 'trickle down'; it is, rather, that more and more people become engaged in the economy, and gain resources as a result. Second, economic development promotes social inclusion. The formal economy does more than promote commerce; it also provides people with resources, communications and extended networks of social contact. This, once again, is not universally positive – the break-up of geographical communities, and the effect that has had on family relationships, has to be counted as part of the cost of growth. Nevertheless, economic development has been one of the principal means of dealing with

social exclusion. Third, economic development promotes equality: as previously
noted (see Box 6 in Chapter Six), developed countries have a rather more equal
distribution of income than countries with limited development. Dollar and
Kraay, for the World Bank, have argued that poor people, in practice, tend to gain
proportionately from the benefits of economic growth. They write:

> Although there is a fair amount of variation about this general
> relationship, a number of popular views about the poverty–growth
> relationship are not true. The effect of growth on the income of the
> poor is no different in poor countries than in rich ones. Incomes of
> the poor do not fall more than proportionately during economic
> crises. The poverty-growth relationship has not changed in recent
> years.[310]

Economic growth does not guarantee that poor people will benefit; some
countries have what Todaro calls 'growth without development'[311], and the
Human Development Index points to a range of cases where human development
is out of step with economic production. The 'variation' referred to by Dollar
and Kraay includes cases where inequality and social conditions have worsened,
as well as cases where they have done better. Overall, however, it is true to say
that economic development reduces poverty.

The second largely successful means of dealing with poverty has been social
protection. In developed economies, the systems which have prevented poverty
most successfully have often been the most generous, and the most expensive.
They provide for material need by offering a high level of material support. The
combination of income maintenance and social services works to prevent people
from falling into poverty. Rather, they protect people's economic position by
income-related provision, preserving people's relative position – and so, a high
degree of inequality – through sickness and old age. That also has the effect of
facilitating social inclusion, because it avoids disruption to social networks. In
the context of developing countries, too, the World Bank argues that social
protection is making a major contribution to the achievement of the Millennium
Development Goals. It does so by facilitating economic development; improving
risk management; decreasing the severity of the experience of poverty; improving
income, with consequent improvements for education and health; and by helping
specific vulnerable groups.[312]

The third most effective approach is political. This is less direct, and possibly
more controversial. If Sen is right, poor people need entitlements. The extension
of the formal economy helps the process, but it is only part of the answer.
Democratic governance is fundamental. This includes not just the democratic
process, but the rule of law, the establishment of individual rights, and the
development of economic and social rights. It may be possible to deal with

poverty without it, but to date it has been part of every approach which has worked.

These three approaches are complementary, rather than contradictory. Political development, as noted in Chapter Ten, goes hand in hand with economic development; the Stalinist position that economic development overrides political rights has been repeatedly exploded, and the development of a political and legal framework is essential for economic prosperity. The assumption that there is a tension between economic performance and social protection is unfounded (see Box 16). There is, then, no reason why these three approaches should not be pursued simultaneously.

Box 16: Welfare expenditure and economic performance

Economic analyses of welfare expenditure tend to offer contradictory predictions about the potential impact of welfare on economic performance. On one hand, it is common to see criticisms implying that welfare expenditure undermines the efficient operation of market economies. Welfare expenditure is believed to have a negative effect on economic performance, either as a drain on public resources or because it 'crowds out' private sector activity. Public sector borrowing crowds out investment, and inflexible labour markets and high social costs lead to the flight of capital. On the other hand, public spending is seen as an economic regulator, stabilising the impact of recession. It enhances human capital, provides support for basic needs and releases resources for consumption. Measures to protect the quality of life, such as policies on crime, health or the role of women, enhance the operation of social relationships and reduce the attendant costs.[313]

To determine what the economic effects really are, it seems appropriate to look at outcomes. In general, richer countries spend a higher proportion of their income on social protection than poorer countries do. That is not surprising; they have more to spend. It is perhaps more useful, then, to focus on countries in similar circumstances, to see whether welfare expenditure actually makes a difference. The graph in Figure 16.1 is based on statistics from the OECD.[314] Each of the points is the position of a country in the OECD in 2001 (with the exceptions of Luxembourg, which is an outlier, and Turkey, for which figures were not available). The longer-established economies tend to be in the upper-right quadrant of the graph, with higher expenditure and higher income.

Figure 16.1: Social expenditure and economic performance

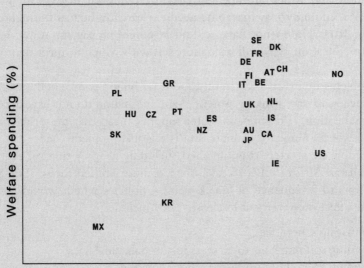

The contention that welfare undermines the economy is not, then, supported by the evidence. One can imagine several lines within the constellation of points, but the truth is that the figures are too diverse to support any firm conclusions. The level of expenditure on social protection is not visibly relevant to the success or failure of an economy.

What is to be done?

There are three main categories of poverty: material need, economic circumstances and social relationships. Here are some modest proposals relating to each of them.

Material need

The first, and most obvious thing that has to be done for the poor is to find ways to meet their material needs. In the developed economies, we tend to think of this in terms of cash support, but for most of the world's poor, that begs many assumptions – cash is only useful in conditions where it can be spent. By contrast, meeting needs in kind, through the provision of goods and services, has immediate benefits and more general implications for needs and resources. Some forms of support have proved to be more acceptable politically than others: providing water or health care, for example, is more widely accepted than providing food or fuel. There are arguments to be held about what kinds of goods are best dealt with publicly, and which are not, but they are not what matters for present purposes; it is enough to say that some needs, at least, can be met through direct provision. If people do not have to find resources to pay for water, health, housing or education, they will have more left with which to meet their other needs.

The problems are massive. Currently, about 1.2 billion people in the world do not have access to safe drinking water, [315] and 3.4 billion do not have access to adequate sanitation. Pressures on water supplies mean that the problems are becoming worse. Similarly, malnutrition is a global problem. More than 850 million people are severely malnourished, including nearly a third of everyone in Sub-Saharan Africa.[316] Let us take, then, a more limited focus. The Sachs report points to a sequence of 'quick wins' – policies which would have an immediate effect on poverty at lost cost. They include:

- eliminating school fees;
- providing soil nutrients to farmers in sub-Saharan Africa;
- providing free school meals for school children;
- supporting breast-feeding;
- deworming school children in affected areas;
- training programmes for community health workers in rural areas;
- providing mosquito nets;
- ending user fees for basic health care in developing countries;
- access to information on sexual and reproductive health;
- drugs for AIDS, tuberculosis and malaria;
- upgrading slums, and providing land for public housing;
- access to electricity, water and sanitation;
- legislation for women's rights, including rights to property;
- action against domestic violence;
- appointing government scientific advisors in every country; and
- planting trees.[317]

The cost of meeting the Millennium Development Goals would be high – it would rise year by year, according to Sachs, from $121 billion in 2006 to $189 billion in 2015.[318] The Jubilee Debt Campaign, more modestly, has made rough estimates for the cost of meeting the Millennium Development Goals in the 39 most highly indebted poor countries. It estimates that the cost of achieving universal primary education would be $6.5 billion; reducing child mortality, improving maternal health and combating the main infectious diseases would cost $20 billion, and halving the proportion of people without safe access to drinking water would cost $2.4 billion.[319] This is not every cost that needs to be met to reduce poverty in these countries – there is also the issue of debt relief, and the larger cost of increasing the incomes of people with the least resources – but this proposal is only concerned, at this point, with initial measures to meet material needs. The point of the limited focus is to show that, despite the size of the problem, a major contribution to world poverty would be both affordable and manageable. By comparison with government expenditure in the OECD countries the costs are, bluntly, trifling.

Economic circumstances

The economic position of the poor is more difficult to deal with directly. The first step is to make economic development possible – removing, for example, the burden of debt repayments, and reviewing the rules that prevent poorer countries from trading on equal terms.[320]

In poor countries, the main problems stem from the under-development of the economy. In developed countries, the core problem is exclusion. Economic development can deal with the former, but not the latter; however successful development may be, some people will be left out. Development is necessary, then, but it is not sufficient. Social protection plays a major role in making resources available and in avoiding the problems of economic exclusion. It is uncertain whether all forms of social protection are equally effective in protecting people against poverty – it has been argued, in the context of developing countries, that support for older people might be less well targeted than support for poor communities.[321] It is clear from the experience of developed economies, however, that 'safety net' provision is not likely to produce adequate coverage in itself, in terms either of the proportion of people covered or of the relative level of benefits.[322] The same must be true of countries in a lesser state of development.

Townsend and Gordon suggest that every country should introduce child benefits as of right.[323] It will be true, in time to come, that we will have to look for ways of giving people everywhere access to cash economies, but it is not going to happen in the foreseeable future. On the general principle that some movement at least needs to be made, we should perhaps look at alternative mechanisms for the distribution of financial and economic support. Foreign aid, the UNDP comments, 'has critical weaknesses – in quantity, equity, predictability and distribution'.[324] The general pattern of foreign aid is that it goes from one government to another; it does not go from a government to people in need in other countries.[325] This is appropriate enough where a country is well governed, but there are many cases where it is not an effective approach, and there is no obvious reason why such a limitation exists. (It is often excused in terms of protocol, but the same obstacles do not exist in relations between developed countries; many governments distribute benefits to former residents living elsewhere in the world.) In principle, governments could provide support direct to people in other countries, as non-governmental organisations currently do, and as individuals do in the form of remittances. The political boundaries are proving to be a major limitation on help for the world's poor.

Social relationships

The third main area to consider is the problem of the social relationships underlying the experience of poverty in different countries. The political and social reforms being fostered by the International Monetary Fund and World Bank are aimed at these issues, and to that extent the obvious issues are being covered – the extension of civil political rights, the establishment of more transparent mechanisms of government, and the encouragement of civil associations. The main outstanding issue these approaches cannot address effectively is the issue of gender. It is difficult to see how the issues can be addressed without establishing rights – one of the 'quick wins' in the Sachs report is to ensure that women have the right to own property – but there are no clear mechanisms by which such rights can be enforced. This has tended to leave international organisations relying on cultural diffusion, or transmitting their values, an approach which is likely to be seen as a covert form of imperialism. An alternative approach has been the use of participatory methods, allowing poor people to identify issues and priorities themselves.

Developing anti-poverty strategies

A strategy to deal with poverty cannot be expected to eliminate every aspect of poverty; it has to be judged by how much it contributes to solutions. Policy does not need to be precise. For practical purposes, anti-poverty policy is best treated as a direction of movement, rather than a set response ('going North' rather than 'going to the North Pole'). Measures help people experiencing poverty if they go in the right direction; they do not help when they go the wrong way. Because we know that people in a range of different circumstances are likely to be poor – like older people, unemployed people or disabled people – we know that measures which help them are also helping to respond to poverty.

For that reason, doing more is better than doing less: the more comprehensive and wide-ranging a strategy can be, the more effect it is likely to have. Some failures have to be expected. The more wide-ranging an anti-poverty strategy is, and certainly the more innovative and ambitious it becomes, the more likely there are to be failures. A good anti-poverty strategy has to try more than it can really deliver.

Poverty refers to far too many issues to be dealt with simply and effectively by a simple set of policies. Complex problems can be dealt with in several ways. One option is to look for a key, finding a simple approach that will deal with lots of problems at once. There are some policies which have a very general effect, and that can help to reduce the scale of the problems that have to be dealt with, but it is improbable that any single measure will deal comprehensively with all the problems. A second is to proceed incrementally – doing what one can, chipping away at the stone, so that large problems become smaller ones. A third approach is to break down complex problems into simpler ones, and to keep breaking them down until each problem is manageable. This is generally good practice, but the range and scope of the problems considered in this book is so wide that it is impossible to deal with them all; there has to be some priority, or at least triage, so that at least a start can be made.

Because poverty is multidimensional, strategy should also be. Michael Lipton argues that anti-poverty strategies have tended to be too complex: 'simple is do-able'.

> Is the process in danger of drowning in alphabet soup, seasoned with initiative overload?[326]

There is an argument for focusing on policies which have a generally beneficial effect, and limited movement is better than none; but most strategies based exclusively on one or two factors have failed, and no single element in policy can possibly deal with all the issues. At the very least, poverty has to be understood as relating to material need, economic circumstances and social relationships: no policy which fails to take each of those into account is going to address the main issues. Strategy needs, for the same reason, to be broadly conceived. Policies which look only at part of the problem might succeed, but they will not satisfy the aspirations and concerns of different people if those concerns are simply ignored.

Another aspect of this is that definitions of poverty need to be inclusive. Because poverty is multifaceted, it is almost never possible to deal with every problem. There has to be some way of deciding priorities, and setting the agenda. One argument for a participative approach to poverty is that the people who experience the problems are best placed to decide what will help the most. Another is that if people's understandings are not taken into account directly, there is a real risk that their problems will not be met at all.

Any anti-poverty strategy is going to miss some aspects of the problem – which means that it must, in some ways at least, be inadequate. But whatever the limitations, something has to be done, and there are policies which can make a positive contribution. It is better, the proverb says, to light a candle than curse the darkness.

Notes

Notes to the Preface

1   D Gordon, R Levitas, C Pantazis, D Patsios, S Payne, P Townsend, L
     Adelman, K Ashworth and S Middleton, 2000, *Poverty and social exclusion
     in Britain*,York: Joseph Rowntree Foundation, www.jrf.org.uk/bookshop/
     eBooks/185935128X.pdf
2   J Moore, 1989, *The end of the line for poverty*, London: Conservative Political
     Centre.

Notes to Chapter One

3   L Wittgenstein, 1958, *The blue and brown books*, Oxford: Blackwell.
4   A Sen, 1981, *Poverty and famines: An essay on entitlement and deprivation*,
     Oxford: Clarendon Press.
5   P Townsend, 1979, *Poverty in the United Kingdom*, Harmondsworth: Penguin;
     P Townsend, 1993, *The international analysis of poverty*, Hemel Hempstead:
     Harvester Wheatsheaf.
6   S Paugam, 2004, *La disqualification sociale*, Paris: Presses Universitaires de
     France.
7   P Townsend et al, 1997, 'An international approach to the measurement
     and explanation of poverty: statement by European social scientists', in
     D Gordon and P Townsend (eds), 2000, *Breadline Europe*, Bristol: The
     Policy Press.
8   D Narayan, 1999, *Voices of the poor: Can anyone hear us?*, Oxford: Oxford
     University Press/World Bank;
     D Narayan, R Chambers, M Shah and P Petesch, 2000, *Voices of the poor:
     Crying out for change*, Oxford: Oxford University Press/World Bank.
9   Dundee Anti Poverty Forum, 2003, *No room for dreams*, Dundee: Dundee
     Anti-Poverty Forum;
     Moray Against Poverty, 2004, *Voices from the edge*, Elgin: MAP.

Notes to Chapter Two

10   UNDP (United Nations Development Programme), 2005, *Human
     development report 2005*, New York: Oxford University Press.

11   M Lipton and M Ravallion, 1995, 'Poverty and policy', in J Behrman and T N Srinivasan (eds) *Handbook of development economics, Volume 3b*, Handbooks in Economics, Volume 9, Amsterdam: Elsevier Science, pp 2551-657.

12   P Townsend, 1985, 'A sociological approach to the measurement of poverty – a rejoinder to Professor Amartya Sen', *Oxford Economic Papers* 37, pp 659-68.

13   OECD (Organisation for Economic Co-operation and Development), 1976, *Public expenditure on income maintenance programmes*, Paris: OECD, p 69.

14   UN (United Nations), 1995, *The Copenhagen Declaration and Program of Action*, New York: UN.

15   UN Human Settlements Programme Global Urban Observatory, 2001, Analysis of urban indicators, http://ww2.unhabitat.org/programmes/guo/guo_analysis.asp

16   UN Human Settlements Programme Global Urban Observatory, 2001, Table 12.

17   A Sen, 1981, *Poverty and famines: An essay on entitlement and deprivation*, Oxford: Clarendon Press.

18   P Townsend, 1979, *Poverty in the United Kingdom*, Harmondsworth: Penguin, p 31.

19   Townsend, 1979, *Poverty in the United Kingdom*, Harmondsworth: Penguin, p 57.

20   P Townsend et al, 1997, 'An international approach to the measurement and explanation of poverty: statement by European social scientists', in D Gordon and P Townsend (eds) 2000, *Breadline Europe*, Bristol: The Policy Press.

21   D Narayan, R Chambers, M Shah and P Petesch, 2000, *Voices of the poor*, New York: World Bank/Oxford University Press.

22   I Garfinkel and S McLanahan, 1988, 'The feminisation of poverty', in D Tomaskovic-Devey (ed) *Poverty and social welfare in the United States*, Boulder, CO: Westview Press;

      J Lewis and D Piachaud, 1992, 'Women and poverty in the twentieth century', in C Glendinning and J Millar, *Women and poverty in Britain in the 1990s*, London: Harvester Wheatsheaf.

23   R Putnam, 2000, *Bowling alone*, New York: Simon and Schuster.

24   D Narayan, R Chambers, M Shah and P Petesch, 2000, *Voices of the poor*, New York: World Bank/Oxford University Press.

Notes to Chapter Three

25   A Sayer, 1981, *Method in social science*, London: Hutchinson.

26   B Seebohm Rowntree, 1901/2000, *Poverty: A study of town life*, Bristol: The Policy Press.

27   J Mack and S Lansley, 1985, *Poor Britain*, London: Allen and Unwin.

28   A Sayer, 1981, *Method in social science*, London: Hutchinson.

29   D Piachaud, 1981, 'Peter Townsend and the Holy Grail', *New Society*, 10 September, p 421.

30   US Department of Health, Education and Welfare, cited in M Carley, 1981, *Social measurement and social indicators*, London: Allen and Unwin.

31   J Brand, 1975, 'The politics of social indicators', *British Journal of Sociology*, 26, pp 78–90.

32   UNDP (United Nations Development Programme), 1999, *Human development report 1999*, New York: Oxford University Press.

33   P Townsend and D Gordon (eds) 2002, *World poverty: New policies to defeat an old enemy*, Bristol: The Policy Press.

34   UNDP (United Nations Development Programme), 2004, *Human development report 2004*, at http://hdr.undp.org/reports/global/2004/pdf/hdr04_HDI.pdf

35   *The Economist*, 2003, 'Epidemics and economics', *The Economist*, 12 April, p 80.

36   Department for Work and Pensions, 2001, *Opportunity for all*, Cm 5260, London: The Stationery Office.

37   www.developmentgoals.com/Poverty.htm#percapita

Notes to Chapter Four

38   UNICEF (United Nations Children's Fund), 2006, *The state of the world's children 2006*, www.unicef.org/sowc06/tables/sowc06_table2.xls

39   J Boltvinik, personal communication.

40   M Brown and N Madge, 1982, *Despite the welfare state*, London: Heinemann Educational Books.

41   P Townsend, 1987, 'Deprivation', *Journal of Social Policy*, 16(2), p 125.

42   International Labour Organization, 1995, 'The framework of ILO action against poverty', in G Rodgers (ed) *The poverty agenda and the ILO*, Geneva: International Institute for Labour Studies, p 6.

43   C Booth, 1902, *Life and labour of the people in London*, Volume 1, London: Macmillan, p 33.

44   P Streeten, 1995, 'Comments on "'The framework of ILO action against poverty'", in G Rodgers (ed) *The poverty agenda and the ILO*, Geneva: International Institute for Labour Studies, p 82.

45   J Mack and S Lansley, 1985, *Breadline Britain*, London: Allen and Unwin.

46   D Piachaud, 1987, 'Problems in the definition and measurement of poverty', *Journal of Social Policy*, 16(2), pp 125–46.

47 D Gordon, R Levitas, C Pantazis, D Patsios, S Payne, P Townsend, L Adelman, K Ashworth and S Middleton, 2000, *Poverty and social exclusion in Britain*, York: Joseph Rowntree Foundation, www.jrf.org.uk/bookshop/eBooks/185935128X.pdf

48 F Coffield and J Sarsby, 1980, *A cycle of deprivation?*, London: Heinemann.

Notes to Chapter Five

49 Social Exclusion Unit, 1998, *Bringing Britain together*, London: The Stationery Office, Table 3.

50 W J Wilson, 1987, *The truly disadvantaged*, Chicago, IL: University of Chicago Press.

51 D Clapham and K Kintrea, 1986, 'Rationing, choice and constraint', *Journal of Social Policy*, 15(1), pp 51-68.

52 S Macintyre, S Maciver and A Sooman, 1993, 'Area, class and health: should we be focusing on places or people?', *Journal of Social Policy*, 22(2), pp 213-34.

53 http://ww2.unhabitat.org/programmes/guo/documents/Table4.pdf

54 For example, O Newman, 1973, *Defensible space: People and design in the violent city*, London: Architectural Press; A Coleman, 1985, *Utopia on trial: Vision and reality in planned housing*, London: Shipman.

55 P Spicker, 1987, 'Poverty and depressed estates: a critique of Utopia on Trial', *Housing Studies*, 2(4), pp 283-92.

56 E Anderson, 1991, 'Neighbourhood effects on teenage pregnancy', and J Crane, 1991, 'Effects of neighborhoods on dropping out of school and teenage childbearing', both in C Jencks and P Peterson (eds) *The urban underclass*, Washington, DC: Brookings.

57 For example, M Bulmer, 1986, *Social science and social policy*, London: Allen and Unwin, ch 11.

58 K Painter, 1992, 'Different worlds', in D Evans, N Fyfe and D Herbert (eds) *Crime, policing and place: Essays in environmental criminology*, London: Routledge, p 182.

59 D Evans, N Fyfe and D Herbert (eds), 1992, *Crime, policing and place: Essays in environmental criminology*, London: Routledge, pp 42-6.

60 C Booth, 1902, *Life and labour of the people in London*, First Series: Poverty, London: Macmillan.

61 P Spicker, 1997, 'Victorian values', in J Goodwin and C Grant (ed) *Built to last?*, London: *Roof Magazine*, pp 17-24.

62 B Seebohm Rowntree, 1901/2000, *Poverty: A study of town life*, Bristol: The Policy Press.

Notes to Chapter Six

63   S Ringen, 1988, 'Direct and indirect measures of poverty', *Journal of Social Policy*, 17(3), p 351.

64   M Brewer, A Goodman and A Leicester, 2006, *Household spending in Britain*, Bristol: The Policy Press.

65   R Titmuss, 1968, *Commitment to welfare*, London: Allen and Unwin, pp 22-3.

66   C Moser, 1998, 'The asset vulnerability framework: reassessing urban poverty reduction strategies', *World Development*, 26(1), pp 1-19.

67   R Putnam, 2000, *Bowling alone*, New York: Simon and Schuster.

68   P Ashton, 1984, 'Poverty and its beholders', *New Society*, 18 October, p 97.

69   M Orshansky, 1965, 'Counting the poor: another look at the poverty profile', *Social Security Bulletin*, 28, pp 3-29.

70   M Lipton, 2001, 'Poverty concepts, policies, partnership and practice', in N Middleton, P O'Keefe and R Visser (eds) *Negotiating poverty*, London: Pluto Press, p 49.

71   For example, R Hauser, H Cremer-Shaefer and U Nouvertné, 1980, *National report on poverty in the Federal Republic of Germany*, Frankfurt: University of Frankfurt;
R Hauser and P Semerau, 1990, 'Trends in poverty and low income in the Federal Republic of Germany 1962/3-1987', in R Teekens and B van Praag (eds) *Analysing poverty in the European Community* (Eurostat News Special Edition 1-1990), Luxembourg: European Communities.

72   For example, G Fisher, 1995, 'Is there such a thing as an absolute poverty line over time?', at http://aspe.hhs.gov/poverty/papers/elassmiv.htm

73   http://hdr.undp.org/statistics/data/indic/indic_137_1_1.html

74   S Samad, 1996, 'The present situation in poverty research', in E Oyen, S Miller and S Samad (eds) *Poverty: A global review*, Oslo: Scandinavian University Press, pp 33-46.

75   G Fields, cited in M Todaro, 1989, *Economic development in the Third World* (3rd edition), Harlow: Longman.

76   M Todaro and S Smith, 2006, *Economic development* (9th edition), Harlow: Pearson, pp 216-18.

77   M O'Higgins and S Jenkins, 1990, 'Poverty in the EC: 1975, 1980, 1985', in R Teekens and B van Praag (eds) *Analysing poverty in the European Community* (Eurostat News Special Edition 1-1990), Luxembourg: European Communities, p 207.

78   International Labour Organization, 1995, 'The framework of ILO action against poverty', in G Rodgers (ed) *The poverty agenda and the ILO*, Geneva: International Institute for Labour Studies, p 6.

79   S Ringen, 1988, 'Direct and indirect measures of poverty', *Journal of Social Policy*, 17(3), pp 351-65.

Notes to Chapter Seven

80   See M Mullard and P Spicker, 1997, *Social policy in a changing society*, London: Routledge, ch 3.

81   DWP (Department for Work and Pensions), 2005, *Low-income dynamics 1991-2003*, London: DWP, at www.dwp.gov.uk/asd/hbai/low_income/paper_M.pdf

82   D Matza and H Miller, 1976, 'Poverty and proletariat', in R Merton and R Nisbet (eds) *Contemporary social problems* (4th edition), New York: Harcourt Brace Jovanovich.

83   L Morris and S Irwin, 1992, 'Employment histories and the concept of the underclass', *Sociology*, 26(3), pp 401-20.

84   P Buhr and S Leibfried, 1995, 'What a difference a day makes', in G Room (ed) *Beyond the threshold*, Bristol: The Policy Press;
R Walker, 1994, *Poverty dynamics*, Aldershot: Avebury;
C Heady, 1997, 'Labour market transitions and social exclusion', *Journal of European Social Policy*, 7(2), pp 119-28.

85   P Townsend, 1979, *Poverty in the United Kingdom*, Harmondsworth: Penguin.

86   J Rex and R Moore, 1967, *Race, community and conflict*, Oxford: Oxford University Press.

87   J Lewis and D Piachaud, 1992, 'Women and poverty in the twentieth century', in C Glendinning and J Millar (eds) *Women and poverty in Britain in the 1990s*, London: Harvester Wheatsheaf.

88   E T Critchlow and E W Hawley, 1989, *Poverty and public policy in modern America*, Chicago, IL: Dorsey;
E Mingione (ed) 1996, *Urban poverty and the underclass*, Oxford: Blackwell;
S Schram, 1995, *Words of welfare*, Minneapolis, MN: University of Minnesota Press.

89   P Spicker, 2002, *Poverty and the welfare state*, London: Catalyst, pp 20-2.

90   For example, G Craig, 1999, 'Race, social security and poverty', in J Ditch (ed) *Introduction to social security*, London: Routledge.

91   T Modood and R Berthoud, 1997, *Ethnic minorities in Britain: Diversity and disadvantage*, London: Policy Studies Institute.

92   T Modood and R Berthoud, 1997, *Ethnic minorities in Britain: Diversity and disadvantage*, London: Policy Studies Institute;
DWP (Department for Work and Pensions), 2005, *Households below average income*, London: DWP, www.dwp.gov.uk/asd/hbai/hbai2005/pdf_files/appendices/appendix_5_hbai06.pdf, table A5 1.3.

93   Fabian Commission on Life Chances and Poverty, 2006, *Narrowing the gap*, London: Fabian Society, p 136.

94   J Millar and C Glendinning, 1989, 'Gender and poverty', *Journal of Social Policy*, 18(3), pp 363-81;
S Payne, 1991, *Women, health and poverty*, London: Harvester Wheatsheaf.

95   See P Townsend, N Davidson and M Whitehead, 1988, *Inequalities in health*, Harmondsworth: Penguin;
      M Bartley, 2004, *Health inequality*, Brighton: Polity.

96   G Smith, D Dorling and M Shaw (eds) 2001, *Poverty, inequality and health in Britain 1800-2000*, Bristol: The Policy Press;
      R Duff and A Hollingshead, 1968, *Sickness and society*, New York: Harper and Row;
      and see eg World Health Organization, 2003, *Social determinants of health: The solid facts*, Copenhagen: WHO, which generalises from the UK to Europe.

97   S Harding, A Bethune, R Maxwell and J Brown, in Department of Health, 1998, *Independent inquiry into inequalities in health*, London: The Stationery Office, table 3, at: www.archive.official-documents.co.uk/document/doh/ih/tab3.htm

98   eg D Gwatkin, S Rustein, K Johnson, R Pande and A Wagstaff, 2001, *Socio-economic differences in health, nutrition and population in India*, Washington DC: World Bank, www-wds.worldbank.org/external/default/W D S C o n t e n t S e r v e r / I W 3 P / I B / 2 0 0 4 / 1 2 / 0 6 / 000012009_20041206145841/Rendered/PDF/305440PAPER0india.pdf

99   M Bonilla-Chacin and J Hammer, 1999, 'Life and death among the poorest', Paper presented at the Economist's Forum, World Bank, April, cited in R Kanbur and L Squire, 1999, 'The evolution of thinking about poverty', at: http://siteresources.worldbank.org/INTPOVERTY/Resources/WDR/evolut.pdf, p 17.

100   For example, in F Field, 1989, *Losing out*, Oxford: Blackwell.

101   K Auletta, 1983, *The underclass*, New York: Vintage Books, p 21.

102   R Lister, 2004, *Poverty*, Brighton: Polity, pp 111-12.

103   R Lister, 1990, *The exclusive society*, London: Child Poverty Action Group;
      C Oppenheim, 1990, *Poverty: The facts*, London: CPAG, p 15.

104   R McGahey, cited in W Wilson, 1987, *The truly disadvantaged*, Chicago, IL: University of Chicago Press, p 6.

105   H Gans, 1990, 'Deconstructing the underclass', *American Planning Association Journal*, 271, cited in F Gaffikin and M Morrissey, 1992, *The new unemployed*, London: Zed Books, p 84.

106   D Matza, 1967, 'The disreputable poor', in R Bendix and S M Lipset (eds) *Class, status and power* (2nd edition), London: Routledge and Kegan Paul.

107   R Lister, 2004, *Poverty*, Brighton: Polity.

108   For example, D Marsden, 1973, *Mothers alone*, Harmondsworth: Penguin, pp 136-8, 175-6;
      or R Titmuss and P Townsend, cited in J MacNicol, 1987, 'In pursuit of the underclass', *Journal of Social Policy*, 16(3), p 300.

109   M Bane and D Ellwood, 1986, 'Slipping into and out of poverty: the dynamics of spells', *Journal of Human Resources*, 21(1) p 21.

110   L Morris, 1994, *Dangerous classes*, London: Routledge.

Notes to Chapter Eight

111   For example, H Silver, 1994, 'Social exclusion and social solidarity: three paradigms', *International Labour Review*, 133(5-6), pp 531-78.

112   N Coote, 1989, 'Catholic social teaching', *Social Policy and Administration*, 23(2), pp 150-60.

113   See M Mauss, 1925/1966, *The gift*, London: Cohen and West.

114   J J Dupeyroux, 1989, *Droit de la sécurité sociale*, Paris: Dalloz, p 286.

115   R Lenoir, 1984, *Les exclus: Un français sur dix*, Paris: Editions du Seuil.

116   S Tiemann, 1993, *Opinion on social exclusion*, OJ 93/C 352/13.

117   R Lenoir, 1974, *Les exclus*, Paris: Editions du Seuil.

118   Cited in A Thévenet, 1986, *L'aide sociale aujourd'hui après la decentralisation*, Paris: Editions ESF, p 320.

119   S C Versele and D van de Velde-Graff, 1976, 'Marginalité ou marginalisation? Accident ou fonction?', *Revue de l'Institut de Sociologie* (1-2), pp 23-49, at pp 26-7.

120   Cited in K Anderson, 1998, *Unlocking the future: Tackling social exclusion*, Edinburgh: Chartered Institute of Housing in Scotland, p 2.

121   S Wuhl, 1992, *Les exclus face à l'emploi*, Paris: Syros Alternatives.

122   E Mossé, 1986, *Les riches et les pauvres*, Paris: Editions du Seuil.

123   Commissariat Général du Plan, 1993, *Cohésion sociale et prévention de l'exclusion*, Paris: La Documentation Française.

124   S. Tiemann, 1993, *Opinion on social exclusion*, OL+J 93/C 352/13.

125   H Silver, 1994, 'Social exclusion and social solidarity: three paradigms', *International Labour Review*, 133(5-6), pp 531-78.

126   Cited in P Vanlerenberghe (chair), 1992, *RMI: Le pari de l'insertion*, Paris: La documentation française, p 115.

127   M Coutinho, 1998, 'Guaranteed minimum income in Portugal and social projects', *Social Services Research* (2), pp 1-10.

128   L Ayala, 1994, 'Social needs, inequality and the welfare state in Spain', *Journal of European Social Policy*, 4(3), pp 159-79.

129   MISEP (European Commission Employment Observatory), 1998, *Policies 64*, Winter, pp 23-4.

130   P Townsend, 1979, *Poverty in the United Kingdom*, Harmondsworth: Penguin, p 31.

131   For example, G Room, 1995, *Beyond the threshold*, Bristol: The Policy Press.

132   Council of the European Communities, 1985, *On specific community action to combat poverty* (Council decision of 19 December 1984), 85/8/EEC, OJ 2/24.

133 Commission of the European Communities, 1993, *Medium term action programme to control exclusion and promote solidarity*, COM(93) 435, p 43.

134 I Kolvin, F Miller, D Scott, S Gatzanis and M Fleeting, 1990, *Continuities of deprivation?*, Aldershot: Avebury.

135 R Walker and K Ashworth, 1994, *Poverty dynamics*, Aldershot: Avebury.

136 Commission of the European Communities, 1993, *Green Paper: European social policy – Options for the Union*, COM (93) final.

137 Commission of the European Communities, 1994, *European social policy – A way forward for the Union* (White Paper), COM (94) 333 final, vol 1, p 37.

138 Commission of the European Communities, 1993, *Green Paper: European Social Policy – Options for the Union*, COM (93) final, p 47.

139 Commission of the European Communities, 1995, *Final report on the implementation of the Community programme concerning the economic and social integration of the economically and socially less privileged groups in society*, COM (95) 94 final, p 12.

140 WHO (World Health Organization), 2000, *ICIDH-2*, Geneva: WHO.

141 For example, M Oliver, 1996, *Understanding disability*, London: Macmillan; P Abberley, 1998, 'The spectre at the feast', in T Shakespeare (ed) *The disability reader*, London: Cassell.

142 WHO (World Health Organization), 2006, 'Burden of disease statistics', at www.who.int/healthinfo/statistics/gbdwhoregionprevalence2002.xls

143 www.who.int/bulletin/volumes/82/11/en/844.pdf

144 E Goffman, 1963, *Stigma*, Harmondsworth: Penguin.

145 See P Spicker, 1984, *Stigma and social welfare*, Beckenham: Croom Helm.

146 M Douglas, 1966, *Purity and danger*, London: Routledge and Kegan Paul.

147 G Orwell, 1937/1959, *The road to Wigan Pier*, London: Secker and Warburg, p 130.

148 M Rokeach and S Parker, 1970, 'Values as social indicators of poverty and race relations in the United States', *The Annals*, 388, pp 97-111.

Notes to Chapter Nine

149 G Simmel, 1908, 'The poor', *Social Problems*, 1965, 13, pp 118-39.

150 Cited in B Cantillon, I Marx and K van den Bosch, 1998, 'Le défi de la pauvreté et de l'exclusion sociale', Paper presented to the International Social Security Association Conference on 'Targeting and Incentives', Jerusalem, January, p 19.

151 E T Critchlow and E W Hawley, 1989, *Poverty and public policy in modern America*, Chicago, IL: Dorsey.

152 I Steizer, 1995, 'American dream lives on', *The Sunday Times*, 15 October, pp 2/11.

153 See N Fraser and L Gordon, 1997, 'Dependency demystified', in R Goodin and P Pettit (eds) *Contemporary political philosophy*, Oxford: Blackwell, p 6181.

154 T Thielke, 2005, 'For God's sake, please stop the aid!', *Der Spiegel*, http://service.spiegel.de/cache/international/spiegel/0,1518,363663,00.html

155 C Murray, 1984, *Losing ground*, New York: Basic Books.

156 L Mead, 1986, *Beyond entitlement*, New York: Free Press.

157 T Alcock, 1752, *Observations on the defects of the Poor Laws*, London: Baldwin and Clements, pp 116–17.

158 H Gascoigne, 1818, *Pauperism*, London: Baldwin, Cradock and Joy, p 8.

159 Earl Grey, 1834, *Corrected report of the speech of the Lord Chancellor in the House of Lords on July 21 1834, on moving the second reading of the Bill to amend the Poor Laws* (2nd edition), London: James Ridgway and Sons, p 20.

160 See for example, P Craig, 1991, 'Costs and benefits', *Journal of Social Policy*, 20(4), pp 537–65;
W van Oorschot, 1995, *Realizing rights*, Aldershot: Avebury;
A Corden, 1999, 'Claiming entitlements', in J Ditch (ed) *Introduction to social security*, London: Routledge.

161 P Spicker, 1984, *Stigma and social welfare*, Beckenham: Croom Helm.

162 A W Gouldner, 1960, 'The norm of reciprocity', *American Sociological Review*, 25(2), pp 161–77.

163 R Pinker, 1971, *Social theory and social policy*, London: Heinemann, p 153.

164 A Walker, 1980, 'The social creation of poverty and dependency in old age', *Journal of Social Policy*, 9(1), pp 49–75.

165 K Carroll, S Murad and J Eliahoo, 2001, 'Stroke incidence and risk factors in a population-based prospective cohort study', *Health Statistics Quarterly*, 12, pp 18–26, available at www.statistics.gov.uk/articles/hsq/HSQ12stroke.pdf

166 C Beatty and S Fothergill, 2003, 'Incapacity Benefits and unemployment', in P Alcock, C Beatty, S Fothergill, R Macmillan and S Yeandle (eds) *Work to welfare*, Cambridge: Cambridge University Press.

167 P Buhr and S Leibfried, 1995, 'What a difference a day makes', in G Room (ed) *Beyond the threshold*, Bristol: The Policy Press;
R Walker, 1994, *Poverty dynamics*, Aldershot: Avebury;
C Heady, 1997, 'Labour market transitions and social exclusion', *Journal of European Social Policy*, 7(2), pp 119–28.

168 DWP (Department for Work and Pensions), 2005, 'Low-income dynamics 1991-2003', London: DWP, available at www.dwp.gov.uk/asd/hbai/low_income_paper_M.pdf

169 L Mead, 1986, Beyond entitlement, New York: Free Press, p 22.

170 L Mead, 1997, *From welfare to work*, London: Institute of Economic Affairs, p 12.

171 A Deacon, 2002, *Perspectives on welfare*, Buckingham: Open University Press.

172 Eurostat, 2006, 'A statistical view of the life of women and men in the EU25', www.lex.unict.it/eurolabor/documentazione/altrestat/eurostat060306.pdf

173 P Spicker, 2005, 'Targeting, residual welfare and related concepts: modes of operation in public policy', *Public Administration*, 83(2), pp 345-65.

174 G Cornia and F Stewart, 1995, 'Food subsidies: two errors of targeting', in F Stewart, *Adjustment and poverty*, London: Routledge.

175 D Coady, M Grosh and J Hoddinott, 2003, *Targeting outcomes redux*, Washington: World Bank, available at www1.worldbank.org/sp/safetynets/Primers/Targerting_Article.pdf (sic), p 38.

Notes to Chapter Ten

176 I Berlin, 1969, *Four essays on liberty*, Oxford: Oxford University Press, pp 122-3.

177 I Berlin, 1969, *Four essays on liberty*, Oxford: Oxford University Press, pp 122-3.

178 J Waldron, 1997, 'Homelessness and the issue of freedom', in R Goodin and P Pettit (eds) *Contemporary political philosophy*, Oxford: Blackwell.

179 See P Spicker, 2006, *Liberty, equality, fraternity*, Bristol: The Policy Press.

180 G Maccallum, 1967, 'Negative and positive freedom', *Philosophical Review*, 76, pp 312-34.

181 A Sen, 1999, *Development as freedom*, Oxford: Clarendon Press.

182 R Lister, 2004, *Poverty*, Brighton: Polity, p 47.

183 http://genderstats.worldbank.org/techPoverty.asp

184 www.developmentgoals.org/Gender_Equality.htm#facts

185 www.worldbank.org/data/wdi2001/pdfs/tab1_3.pdf

186 www.worldbank.org/data/wdi2001/pdfs/tab1_3.pdf

187 www.worldbank.org/data/wdi2001/pdfs/tab1_3.pdf

188 A Sen, 1981, *Poverty and famines: An essay on entitlement and deprivation*, Oxford: Clarendon Press.

189 J Dreze and A Sen, 1989, *Hunger and public action*, Oxford: Clarendon Press.

190 D Narayan, R Chambers, M Shah and P Petesch, 2000, *Voices of the poor*, New York: World Bank/Oxford University Press.

191 J Handler, 1972, *Reforming the poor*, New York: Basic Books, p 24.

192 R Goodin and J Le Grand, 1987, *Not only the poor*, London: Allen and Unwin.

193 A Sen, 2002, 'Why half the planet is hungry', *The Observer*, 16 June.

194 E Burke, 1790/1959, *Reflections on the revolution in France*, New York: Holt, Rinehart and Winston, p 71.

195 D Green, 1993, *Reinventing civil society*, London: Institute of Economic Affairs.

196 See P Spicker, 2000, *The welfare state: A general theory*, London: Sage Publications.

Notes to Chapter Eleven

197 M Sahlins, 1974, *Stone age economics*, London: Tavistock.

198 N Coote, 1989, 'Catholic social teaching', *Social Policy and Administration*, 23(2), pp 150-60.

199 P Spicker, 2001, 'The rights of the poor', in P Robson and A Kjonstad (eds) *Poverty and the law*, Oxford: Hart.

200 M Mauss, 1925/1966, *The gift: Forms and functions of exchange in archaic societies*, London: Cohen and West;
A Gouldner, 1960, 'The norm of reciprocity', *American Sociological Review*, 25(2), pp 161-77.

201 See P Spicker, 2006, *Liberty, equality, fraternity*, Bristol: The Policy Press.

202 UNCHR, 2006, 'Global refugee trends 2005', at www.unhcr.org/cgi-bin/texis/vtx/statistics/opendoc.pdf?tbl=STATISTICS&id=4486ceb12

203 Cited in G Bowpitt, 1985, 'Secularisation and the origins of professional social work in Britain', PhD thesis, University College of Swansea, p 379.

204 B Seebohm Rowntree, 1901/2000, *Poverty: A study of town life*, Bristol: The Policy Press, pp 133-4.

205 Tony Blair, at http://news.bbc.co.uk/hi/english/events/newsnight/newsid_1372000/1372220.stm

206 J Moore, 1989, *The end of the line for poverty*, London: Conservative Political Centre.

207 K Joseph and R Sumption, 1979, *Equality*, London: John Murray.

208 Honorius III, 1217, cited in Ordo Praedicatorum, 'The vow of poverty', at www.op.org/curia/JPC/booklets/jp0105.htm

209 For example, D Craik, 1856, *John Halifax, gentleman*, London: Dent.

210 M Stewart, 1973, *Keynes and after*, Harmondsworth: Penguin.

211 H Spencer, 1851, *Social statics*, London: John Chapman.

Notes to Chapter Twelve

212 E Banfield, 1968, *The unheavenly city*, Boston, MA: Little Brown, p 62.

213 C Murray, 1989, 'Underclass', *The Sunday Times Magazine*, 26 November, p 26.

214 P Cull, 2005, 'Government has eye on weeding out grant cheats', *The Herald Online*, www.theherald.co.za/herald/2005/09/08/news/n24%5F08092005.htm

215 For example, T Gladwin, 1967, *Poverty USA*, Boston, MA: Little Brown; S Damer, 1989, *From Moorepark to 'Wine Alley': The rise and fall of a Glasgow housing scheme*, Edinburgh: Edinburgh University Press.

216 P Townsend, 1979, *Poverty in the United Kingdom*, Harmondsworth: Penguin.

217 C Murray, 1984, *Losing ground*, New York: Basic Books.

218 A Atkinson, 1990, *Institutional features of unemployment insurance and the working of the labour market*, London: Suntory-Toyota Centre for Economics and Related Disciplines, p 2.

219 O Lewis, 1964, *The children of Sanchez*, Harmondsworth: Penguin; O Lewis, 1968, *La vida*, London: Panther.

220 See J Hill, 1978, 'The psychological impact of unemployment', *New Society*, 43, 19 January, pp 118-20; N Wansborough, 1980, 'Absence makes the heart grow fainter', *New Society*, 51, 3 January, pp 16-17.

221 W Haggstrom, 1964, 'The power of the poor', in F Riessman, J Cohen and A Pearl (eds) *Mental health of the poor*, New York: Free Press.

222 I Sawhill et al, 1987, cited in S McLanahan and I Garfinkel, 1989, 'Single mothers, the underclass and social policy', *Annals of the American Academy of Political and Social Sciences*, 501, pp 92-104, p 94.

223 See M Flynn, P Flynn and N Mellor, 1972, 'Social malaise research', *Social Trends 6*, pp 43-8; Nottinghamshire Planning Department, 1983, *Disadvantage in Nottinghamshire: County Deprived Area Study 1983*, Nottingham: Nottinghamshire County Council; and, for an interpretation, P Spicker, 1987, 'Poverty and depressed estates', *Housing Studies*, 2(4), pp 283-92.

224 For example, D Byrne, S Harrison, J Keithley and P McCarthy, 1986, *Housing and health*, Aldershot: Gower; S Platt, C Martin and S Hunt, 1990, 'The mental health of women with children living in deprived areas of Great Britain', in D Goldberg and D Tantam (eds) *The public health impact of mental disorder*, Toronto: Hogrefe and Huber.

225 S Platt, C Martin and S Hunt, 1990, 'The mental health of women with children living in deprived areas of Great Britain', in D Goldberg and D Tantam (eds) The *public health impact of mental disorder*, Toronto: Hogrefe and Huber, p 133.

226   Note previous references to K Auletta, 1983, *The underclass*, New York: Vintage Books, p 21;

C Murray, 1989, 'Underclass', *The Sunday Times Magazine*, 26 November, p 26;

L Mead, 1997, *From welfare to work*, London: Institute of Economic Affairs, p 12.

227   J Ladanyi, 1992, 'Where criminals live: a study of Budapest', in D Evans, N Fyfe and D Herbert (eds) *Crime, policing and place: Essays in environmental criminology*, London: Routledge.

228   D Downes, 1993, 'Broken windows of opportunity: crime, inequality and unemployment', Paper presented to the Social Policy Association Conference, University of Liverpool, July.

229   N Pleace, 1998, 'Single homelessness as social exclusion', *Social Policy and Administration*, 32(1), pp 46-59.

230   G Velho, 1978, 'Stigmatisation and deviance in Copacabana', *Social Problems*, 25(5), pp 526-30.

231   E Banfield, 1968, *The unheavenly city*, Boston, MA: Little Brown.

232   A Coleman, 1985, *Utopia on trial: Vision and reality in planned housing*, London: Shipman.

233   S Box, 1987, *Recession, crime and punishment*, London: Macmillan, p 87.

234   N Dennis, 1997, *The invention of permanent poverty*, London: IEA Health and Welfare Unit.

235   R Lampard, 1994, 'An examination of the relationship between marital dissolution and unemployment', in D Gallie, C Marsh and C Vogler (eds) *Social change and the experience of unemployment*, Oxford: Oxford University Press;

K Kiernan and V Estaugh, 1993, research cited in *The Guardian*, 'Parents who cohabit poorer than those who marry', 1 June, p 4.

236   B Gillam, 1997, *The facts about teenage pregnancies*, London: Cassell.

237   I Allen and S Dowling, 1998, *Teenage mothers: Decisions and outcomes*, London: Policy Studies Institute;

S Cater and L Coleman, 2006, *'Planned' teenage pregnancy: Perspectives of young parents from disadvantaged backgrounds*, Bristol/York: The Policy Press/ Joseph Rowntree Foundation.

238   R Jarrett, 1994, 'Living poor: family life among single parent African American women', *Social Problems*, 41(1), p 38.

Notes to Chapter Thirteen

239   R J Herrnstein and C Murray, 1994, *The bell curve: Intelligence and class structure in American life*, New York: Free Press.

240   M Brown and N Madge, 1982, *Despite the welfare state*, London: Heinemann.

241   I Kolvin, F J W Miller, D M Scott, S R M Gatzanis and M Fleeting, 1990, *Continuities of deprivation?: The Newcastle 1000 family study*, Aldershot: Avebury.

242   M Corcoran and A Chaudry, cited in F McCoull and J Pech, 2000, 'Transgenerational income support dependence in Australia', in P Saunders (ed) *Reforming the Australian welfare state*, Melbourne: Australian Institute of Family Studies, p 94.

243   C Valentine, 1968, *Culture and poverty*, Chicago, IL: University of Chicago Press, p 5.

244   D Matza, 1967, 'The disreputable poor', in R Bendix and S M Lipset (eds) *Class, status and power* (2nd edition), London: Routledge and Kegan Paul.

245   O Lewis, 1968, *La vida*, London: Panther, p 53.

246   O Lewis, 1968, *La vida*, London: Panther, p 144.

247   T W Adorno, E Frenkel-Brunswick, D J Levinson and R N Sandford, 1969, *The authoritarian personality*, New York: Norton.

248   R Lampard, 1994, 'An examination of the relationship between marital dissolution and unemployment', in D Gallie, C Marsh and C Vogler (eds) *Social change and the experience of unemployment*, Oxford: Oxford University Press;
K Kiernan and G Mueller, 1998, *The divorced and who divorces?*, London: London School of Economics and Political Science.

249   M Sullivan, 1989, 'Absent fathers in the inner city', *Annals of the American Academy of Political and Social Science*, 501, pp 48-58.

250   T R Malthus, 1798-1973, *An essay on the principle of population*, London: Dent.

251   See, for example, S McDaniel, 1990, 'People pressure', in C Mungall and D McLaren (eds) *Planet under stress*, Toronto: Oxford University Press ;
D H Meadows, D L Meadows and J Randers, 1992, *Beyond the limits*, London: Earthscan.

252   D H Meadows et al, 1972, *Limits to growth*, London: Earth Island.

253   For example, S McDaniel, 1990, 'People pressure', in C Mungall and D McLaren (eds) *Planet under stress*, Toronto: Oxford University Press;
D H Meadows, D L Meadows and J Randers, 1992, *Beyond the limits*, London: Earthscan.

254   J Cohen, 1995, *How many people can the earth support?*, New York: Norton.

255   UNICEF (United Nations Children's Fund), 2004, 'The state of the world's children 2005', at www.unicef.org/sowc05/english/Table6_E.xls

256   Cited in K Gulhati and L Bates, 1994, 'Developing countries and the international population debate', in R Cassen (ed) *Population and development: Old debates, new conclusions*, Washington, DC: Overseas Development Council, p 53.

257   H Spencer, 1851, *Social statics*, London: John Chapman.

258   For example, C Murray, 1984, *Losing ground*, New York: Basic Books; L Mead, 1992, *The new politics of poverty*, New York: Basic Books.

259   See R Goodin, B Headey, R Muffels and H-J Dirven, 2000, *The real worlds of welfare capitalism*, Cambridge: Cambridge University Press.

Notes to Chapter Fourteen

260   D Gordon and P Spicker (eds) 1997, *The international glossary on poverty*, London: Routledge, pp 102-3.

261   A B Atkinson, 1998, *Poverty in Europe*, Oxford: Blackwell, p 44.

262   W Rostow, 1962, *The stages of economic growth*, Cambridge: Cambridge University Press.

263   See UNDP (United Nations Development Programme), 2005, *Human development report 2005*, New York: Oxford University Press, table 14, at http://hdr.undp.org/reports/global/2005/pdf/HDR05_HDI.pdf

264   M Todaro and S Smith, 2006, *Economic development* (9th edition), Harlow: Pearson, p 73.

265   J Hecht, 2006, 'Disappearing deltas could spell disaster', *New Scientist*, 20 February.

266   UN Millennium Project, 2005, *Investing in development*, New York: United Nations Development Programme, pp 176-7.

267   WHO (World Health Organization), 2005, *World health report 2005*, at www.who.int/whr/2005/en/index.html

268   WHO (World Health Organization), 2004, *World health report 2004*, at www.who.int/whr/2004/annex/topic/annex3.xls

269   WHO (World Health Organization), 2004, 'Poverty Reduction Strategy Papers: their significance for health', at www.who.int/trade/en/PRSP1.pdf

270   M Todaro and S Smith, 2006, *Economic development* (9th edition), Harlow: Pearson, pp 602-3.

271   See UNDP, 2005, *Human development report 2005*, New York: Oxford University Press, table 1, at: http://hdr.undp.org/reports/global/2005/pdf/HDR05_HDI.pdf

272   Cited in M Todaro, 1989, *Economic development in the Third World* (3rd edition), Harlow: Longman, p 144.

273   M Todaro, 1989, *Economic development in the Third World* (3rd edition), Harlow: Longman, pp 169-70.

274   D Dollar and A Kraay, 2000, 'Growth is good for the poor', at www.worldbank.org/research/growth/pdfiles/growthgoodforpoor.pdf

275   www.imf.org/external/np/prsp/prsp.asp

276   M Todaro and S Smith, 2006, *Economic development* (9th edition), Harlow: Pearson, pp 119-22.

277   M Messkoub, 1992, 'Deprivation and structural adjustment', in M Wuyts, M Mackintosh and T Hewitt (eds) *Development policy and public action*, Oxford: Oxford University Press.

278   K Donkor, 2002, 'Structural adjustment and mass poverty in Ghana', in P Townsend and D Gordon (eds) *World poverty*, Bristol: The Policy Press.

279   For example, J Sachs, 2005, *The end of poverty*, New York: Penguin.

280   see World Bank Governance Data, at www.worldbank.org/wbi/governance/data.html#dataset2001

281   For example, M Lundberg and P Diskin, 1995, 'Targeting assistance to the poor and food insecure', US Agency for International Development, at: www.afr-sd.org/publications/9target.pdf

282   W Savedoff and K Hussmann, 2006, 'Why are health systems prone to corruption?', in Transparency International, *Global Corruption Report 2006*, at www.transparency.org/content/download/4816/28503/file/Part%201_1_causes%20of%20corruption.pdf

283   See Transparency International, 2005, 'Corruption Perceptions Index', at: www.transparency.org/policy_research/surveys_indices/cpi/2005

284   S Hawley, 1999, 'Exporting corruption: privatization, multinationals and bribery', Corner House Briefing 19, at www.thecornerhouse.org.uk/item.shtml?x=51975

285   R Titmuss, 1963, 'War and social policy', in *Essays on the 'welfare state'*, London: Allen and Unwin;
H Wilensky, 1975, *The welfare state and equality*, Berkeley, CA: University of California Press.

286   M Todaro and S Smith, 2006, *Economic development* (9th edition), Harlow: Pearson, pp 770-74.

287   UN Millennium Project, 2005, *Investing in development: Overview*, New York: United Nations Development Programme, p 8.

288   Oxfam International, 2002, *Rigged rules and double standards*, Oxford: Oxfam International.

289   UNDP (United Nations Development Programme), 2005, *Human development report 2005*, New York: Oxford University Press, p 10.

290   For example, M Todaro and S Smith, 2006, *Economic development* (9th edition), Harlow: Pearson, pp 654-8.

291   Action Aid, CAFOD, Oxfam, 2005, 'Do the deal', at www.oxfam.org.uk/what_we_do/issues/debt_aid/downloads/g7_deal.pdf

292   M Todaro and S Smith, 2006, *Economic development* (9th edition), Harlow: Pearson, pp 673-80.

293   G Brown, 2000, 'Gilbert Murray Memorial Lecture', at www.oxfam.org.uk/what_we_do/issues/debt_aid/speech_gordonbrown.htm

294   E Oyen, 2002, 'Poverty production', at www.crop.org/publications/files/report/Poverty_production.pdf

295   D Simon (ed) 2006, *Fifty key thinkers on development*, London: Routledge.

296   D Lal, 1997, *The poverty of 'development economics'*, London: Institute of Economic Affairs.

297   Smith, cited in D Lal, 1997, *The poverty of 'development economics'*, London: Institute of Economic Affairs, p 44.

Notes to Chapter Fifteen

298   J Stryker, 2001, 'Common diagnostic framework for poverty reduction', in N Middleton, P O'Keefe and R Visser (eds) *Negotiating poverty*, London: Pluto Press.

299   See, for example, D Mitchell, 1991, *Income transfers in ten welfare states*, Aldershot: Avebury.

300   T M Smeeding, M O'Higgins and L Rainwater (eds), 1990 *Poverty, inequality and income distribution in comparative perspective*, New York: Harvester Wheatsheaf.

301   G Esping-Andersen, 1990, *The three worlds of welfare capitalism*, Brighton: Polity;
      R Goodin, B Headey, R Muffels and H-J Dirven, 2000, *The real worlds of welfare capitalism*, Cambridge: Cambridge University Press.

302   For example, H Boies, 1893, *Prisoners and paupers*, New York: Knickerbocker Press;
      and see D Pick, 1989, *Faces of degeneration*, Cambridge: Cambridge University Press.

303   See E Carlson, 2001, *The unfit*, New York: Cold Spring Harbor Laboratory Press.

304   R Talmy, 1962, *Histoire du mouvement familial en France 1896-1939*, Paris: Union Nationale des Caisses d'Allocations Familiales.

305   www.un.org/millenniumgoals/

306   UN Millennium Project, 2005, *Investing in development: Overview*, New York: United Nations Development Programme.

307   http://millenniumindicators.un.org/unsd/mi/mi_goals.asp

Notes to Chapter Sixteen

308   R Mishra, 1994, 'The study of poverty in North America', CROP/UNESCO Symposium on: Regional State-of-the-art Reviews on Poverty Research, Paris, 30 November-2 December.

309   D Macarov and J Dixon, 1998, 'Poverty in review', *Poverty: A persistent global reality*, London: Routledge, pp 274-5.

310   D Dollar and A Kraay, 2000, 'Growth is good for the poor', at www.worldbank.org/research/growth/pdfiles/growthgoodforpoor.pdf

311 M Todaro and S Smith, 2006, *Economic development* (9th edition), Harlow: Pearson, ch 2.

312 World Bank, 2003, 'The contribution of social protection to the Millennium Development Goals', at http://siteresources.worldbank.org/SOCIALPROTECTION/Publications/20847137/SPMDGs.pdf

313 C Hay, 2001, 'Globalisation, economic change and the welfare state', in R Sykes, B Palier and P Prior (eds) *Globalization and European welfare states*, Basingstoke: Palgrave.

314 OECD, 2006, *OECD Factbook 2006*, at http://puck.sourceoecd.org/vl=775315/cl=24/nw=1/rpsv/factbook/; http://hdr.undp.org/reports/global/2003/pdf/hdr03_HDI.pdf, pp 237-28

315 www.developmentgoals.com/Environment.htm#cleanwater

316 FAO (Food and Agriculture Organization) of the United Nations, 2004, *The state of food insecurity in the world 2004*, Rome: FAO, pp 34-6.

317 UN Millennium Project, 2005, *Investing in development: Overview*, New York: United Nations Development Programme, p 26.

318 UN Millennium Project, 2005, *Investing in development: Full report*, New York: United Nations Development Programme, p 251.

319 R Greenhill, 2002, *The unbreakable link: Debt relief and the millennium development goals*, London: New Economics Foundation/Jubilee Debt Campaign, p 18.

320 K Watkins, 2002, *Rigged rules and double standards: Trade, globalisation and the fight against poverty*, Oxford: Oxfam International.

321 D Coady, M. Grosh and J. Hoddinott, 2003, *Targeting outcomes redux*, Washington: World Bank, www1.worldbank.org/sp/safetynets/Primers/Targerting_Article.pdf (sic), p 38.

322 D Mitchell, 1991, *Income transfers in ten welfare states*, Aldershot: Avebury.

323 P Townsend and D Gordon, 2002, *World poverty*, Bristol: The Policy Press, p 433.

324 Cited in M Todaro, 1994, *Economic development* (5th edition), New York: Longmans, p 526.

325 J Eaton, 1995, 'Foreign public capital flows', in J Behrman and T Srinivasan (eds) *Handbook of development economics*, Volume 3B, Elsevier: Amsterdam.

326 M Lipton, 2001, 'Poverty concepts, policies, partnership and practice', in N Middleton, P O'Keefe and R Visser (eds) *Negotiating poverty*, London: Pluto Press, p 51.

Index

A

absolute poverty 11-14, 15, 16, 29, 31
agency explanations for poverty 111, 117-8, 130-1
aid (overseas development assistance) 131, 138, 139, 149
anti-poverty strategies *see* responses to poverty; strategic intervention
areas and area deprivation 15, 37-42, 56, 105
armed conflict 124, 128-9, 130
assets 46, 58

B

basic needs 12-13, 29
basic security 5, 17, 89
benefits iv, 54, 55, 67-8, 73, 77, 78, 79, 80, 102, 138, 143-4, 149 *see* safety net; social protection
Booth, Charles 35, 41-2, 95
Breadline Britain 19, 31, 32, 35-6
budget standards *see* household budgets

C

capabilities 14, 17
Catholic social teaching 65, 93, 138
characteristics 14
charity 55, 87, 93, 94, 101
claims 29-30
class 53-61, 105
  economic class 4, 6
  social class 4, 6, 53, 55
colonialism and neo-colonialism 130
command over resources 45-6, 52
commodities 14
comparisons between rich and poor countries 11-17, 48
conditionality 131
consensual measures 19 *see Breadline Britain*
consumption 34, 45-6, 51-52
corporatism 127
corruption 74, 118, 127-8, 131
crime 41, 105-6
culture of poverty 78, 104, 113-5
cycle of deprivation 112

D

DALY (Disability Adjusted Life Year) 124
debt 67, 129-130, 139, 148, 149
definitions of poverty 3-10

D (continued)

degeneracy 137 *see* genetic explanations
democracy 86, 88-9, 126, 140, 145
dependency 4, 6, 73-81, 104, 131-2, 140
dependency culture 74-5, 77-8
deprivation v, 4, 6, 31-6
  multiple deprivation 35-6
destitution 33
development 23, 53, 121-132, 145, 149 *see* economic growth; human development
'direct' and 'indirect' measures 45, 52
dirigisme 126
disability 55, 69-70, 124
disadvantage 34, 111, 117 *see* inequality
dynamics of poverty 54, 60-1, 69, 78

E

economic circumstances 6, 7, 43-59, 149
economic distance 4, 5, 6, 49, 50-1, 52, 97
economic growth 21, 23, 99, 115-6, 122, 140, 145
education 22, 48, 85, 139, 148
empowerment 8, 84-6
entitlement 5, 6, 86-7, 145
environmental factors 39
European Union (EU) 5, 66-69, 129
exclusion 5, 6, 65-72, 97, 136, 149
expenditure 45-6
explanations for poverty 109-132
extensive research 19

F

familial explanations for poverty 111, 119
family relationships 31, 46, 107, 112, 113-5
famine 86, 88
freedom 83-4, 87, 89
food iv, v, 4, 7, 9, 12, 14, 29-35 *passim*, 48, 50, 53, 88, 98, 115, 135-6, 147 *see* malnutrition
formal economy 51, 53-5, 79, 125, 127, 131, 144-145
functionalism 117

G

gender 15-16, 22, 56, 79, 85, 150
genetic explanations for poverty 112, 118-9, 137
GDP (Gross Domestic Product) 22, 23, 54, 125

H

health 7, 12, 16, 20–3 *passim*, 31, 33, 38, 39, 48, 57–9, 66, 67, 69–70, 77, 97, 98, 105, 123–4, 139, 145, 148
  health care 48, 50, 88, 90, 123, 128, 136, 137, 139, 144, 147, 148
HIPCs (heavily indebted poor countries) 121, 131 *see* debt
homelessness 12–14, 35, 50, 55, 84, 87, 106
household budgets 7, 19, 34, 42, 48, 96
housing v, 13, 15, 38–9, 46, 50, 106
  housing classes 55
human development 124–5
  Human Development Index (HDI) 21, 22, 23, 51
Human Poverty Index (HPI) 11

I

incentives to work 99, 103, 140
income 6, 23, 25, 34, 37, 45–52, 58
indicators 20–6, 97
  headline indicators 26, 28
  multiple indicators 24–5
  summary indices 23–4
inequality iv, 14, 15, 20, 21, 22, 49–51, 58, 69, 83, 97, 106, 117, 127, 140
intensive research 19
intergenerational continuity 112–13
International Declaration 6, 15, 47
International Monetary Fund (IMF) 125, 127, 131, 138, 150
international trade 129, 139, 149

K

Keynesianism 99, 126, 137, 140, 143

L

labour markets 40, 54–55, 61, 79, 85
  dual labour market 54
  marginal employment 54, 81
  sub-employment 54, 61
  see unemployment
land 13, 15, 125
Least Developed Countries (LDCs) 121, 139
liberal economics 126–7
liberty *see* freedom

M

malnutrition 30, 57, 139, 148
Malthusianism 115–6
marginality 66, 69, 105, 107, 112
Marxist views 53, 59, 117
material need 4, 6, 7, 27–42, 147–9
meaning of poverty iv, 3–10

means tests 80–1, 102, 127
measurement 21, 23–4
median income 22, 49, 54, 97
migrants 72, 94, 95, 129
Millennium Development Goals (MDGs) 138, 145, 148
minority ethnic groups 56, 112
moral condemnation of poverty v–vi, 71–2, 73–8, 101–8, 118–20
mortality 20, 21, 23, 25, 58, 115–16, 123, 139, 148
multi-dimensional views 7–10, 23, 25, 150–1
multinational corporations *see* transnational companies

N

natural resources 115–16, 122–3
needs 6, 12, 15, 29–36
normative view of poverty v–vi, 5, 6, 20, 56–7, 93–99
norms 12–13, 14, 15, 24, 48, 97

O

OECD (Organization for Economic Cooperation and Development) countries 73–4, 146–7, 149
opportunities iv, v, 4, 9, 30, 55–7, 61, 83, 102, 107, 112, 117
Overseas Development Assistance *see* aid

P

participation in society iv, 5, 12, 15, 16, 17, 47, 68–9, 97, 98, 111, 114, 125
participatory research 8–10, 19, 85
pathological explanations 111–12, 118
patterns of deprivation 4, 6, 34–6
police 17, 87, 106, 126
Poor Law 71, 73, 75, 78, 80, 90, 103, 136–7, 140, 145
poor relief 135–6
population 116–7
power 4, 7, 17, 84–6, 88, 117, 121
poverty dominance 121
poverty goods 50
poverty line 42
  US poverty line 47, 48, 50
poverty production 130
Poverty Reduction Strategy Papers (PRSPs) 125–6, 127, 131, 138, 140–1
precariousness 15
prevention 137
prices 48, 50
primary poverty 35, 96
property rights 13, 15, 125
purchasing power parity 48

Q

"quick wins" 148, 150

R

'race' 56, 69, 112, 138 *see* minority ethnic groups; genetic explanations
reciprocity 76, 94
refugees *see* migrants
relative deprivation 5, 15, 29
relative poverty 11, 14-15, 16, 29, 97
remittances 95, 129, 149
revenu minimum d'insertion (RMI) 67-8
resource-based explanations for poverty 111, 115-16 *see* natural resources
resources 4, 6, 33, 45-52, 55
responses to poverty 133-51
rights 13, 86-8, 89, 93-4, 140
Rowntree, B Seebohm 19, 34-5, 42, 95-6

S

safety net 90, 136, 149
scientific approaches 6-7, 8
selectivity 80, 143-4
Sen, Amartya 5, 14, 85, 86-7, 88, 89, 145
single parents 37, 77, 107
slums 38, 106, 148
social capital 46
social disqualification 5
social inclusion 65, 67-8, 81
social problems 105-6
social protection 78, 87, 89-90, 136, 149
social relationships v, 6, 7, 15, 17, 39, 46, 63-90, 150
solidarity 65, 68, 78, 94, 101
Stalinism 126, 146
standard of living 4, 6, 34-5, 52
stigma 60, 71-2, 76-7
strategic intervention 136-7, 139-141, 150-1
structural adjustment 127
structural dependency 77, 118, 131-2
structural explanations 105-6, 117
sub-cultural explanations 111, 119 *see* culture of poverty

T

targeting 80, 127, 135
targets 139, 141
teenage pregnancy 39, 101, 107, 111-2
Townsend, Peter 5, 12, 15, 19-20, 21, 33, 34, 55, 68, 102, 149

transmitted deprivation *see* intergenerational continuity
transnational companies 128, 131

U

U curve 51
underclass 59-60, 66, 69, 78, 104-5, 113
unemployment 37, 66-7, 77, 79, 104, 107, 137 *see* labour market
United Nations (UN) 5, 85, 94, 131
United Nations Development Programme (UNDP) 11, 14, 21, 22, 48, 129, 149
universality 80

V

Voices of the poor 8, 9, 15-6, 19, 87, 106
voluntary poverty 97-8
vulnerability 35, 37, 53, 123, 127

W

war *see* armed conflict
wealth 45-6, 58
web of deprivation 36, 57
Weberian approaches 53, 55, 59, 67
welfare rights 87
welfare expenditure 146-7
welfare states 89, 117-18, 146-7
women 13, 56, 148 *see* gender
World Health Organization (WHO) 69-70, 124
World Bank 8, 21, 25, 47, 48, 50, 85, 121, 125, 127, 131, 145, 150

Other titles by Paul Spicker available from The Policy Press

Liberty, equality, fraternity

Paul Spicker's new book takes the three founding principles of the French Revolution – Liberty, Equality, Fraternity – and examines how they relate to social policy today.

The book considers the political and moral dimensions of a wide range of social policies, and offers a different way of thinking about the subject from the way it is usually analysed.

The book is in three main parts, devoted to Liberty, Equality and Fraternity in turn. Each part explores the elements and dimensions of the key concept, its application to policy, its interrelationship with the other two principles, and how policies have developed to promote the principle in society. The conclusion outlines three models of radical politics, based on the main concepts.

Hardback £50.00 US$95.00 **ISBN-10** 1 86134 841 X **ISBN-13** 978 1 86134 841 8
234 x 156mm 208 pages September 2006

LIBERTY, EQUALITY, FRATERNITY
Paul Spicker

Policy analysis for practice
Applying social policy

People who work in planning, management and service delivery in the public sector need to know how policy is translated into practice, what is happening, and whether a policy works. *Policy analysis for practice* introduces students and practitioners to the concepts, methods and techniques required to undertake the analysis and review of policy and its implementation. Focusing on developing understanding and skills for a growing area of practice, it combines material from public and social administration with examples and application to social policy and the social services.

Paperback £16.99 US$29.95 **ISBN-10** 1 86134 825 8 **ISBN-13** 978 1 86134 825 8
Hardback £55.00 US$89.95 **ISBN-10** 1 86134 826 6 **ISBN-13** 978 1 86134 826 5
234 x 156mm 216 pages June 2006

To order copies of these publications or any other Policy Press titles please visit **www.policypress.org.uk** or contact:

In the UK and Europe:
Marston Book Services,
PO Box 269, Abingdon,
Oxon, OX14 4YN, UK
Tel: +44 (0)1235 465500
Fax: +44 (0)1235 465556
Email: direct.orders@marston.co.uk

In the USA and Canada:
ISBS, 920 NE 58th Street, Suite
300, Portland,
OR 97213-3786, USA
Tel: +1 800 944 6190
(toll free)
Fax: +1 503 280 8832
Email: info@isbs.com

**In Australia and
New Zealand:**
DA Information Services,
648 Whitehorse Road Mitcham,
Victoria 3132, Australia
Tel: +61 (3) 9210 7777
Fax: +61 (3) 9210 7788
E-mail: service@dadirect.com.au